FLETCHER ON PERFECTION

by
JOHN FLETCHER

Compiled by
THOMAS RUTHERFORD

Edited by
MICHAEL R. WILLIAMS

SCHMUL PUBLISHING C
SCHMUL'S WESLEYAN BOOK CLUB   SALEM,

Published by Schmul Publishing Co.
PO Box 716
Salem, Ohio 44460

Printed in the United States of America

Printed by Old Paths Tract Society
RR2, Box 43
Shoals, Indiana 47581

ISBN 0-88019-405-7

Contents

Foreword

THERE ARE FEW THINGS that elicit more skepticism, arouse more antagonism and are less understood than the doctrine of Christian perfection. This fact has become even more apparent , it seems, in the last twenty-five years. Indeed, the very thought of perfection is met with a certain incredulity on the part of many professed Christians. Yet we who not only firmly believe it to be thoroughly scriptural, but seek to faithfully live such a life, and thereby persuade others of the joyous reality of this experience of perfect love and obedience, must be thoroughly grounded in the doctrine. Too often we have sallied forth without the armor of a coherent, consistent theology and have been discomfited in the fray. What better remedy than to return to our spiritual fathers who not only extracted the ore from the biblical mine but also refined it and fashioned it into a complete body armor that may withstand the assaults of all opponents.

John Fletcher is one of those who ranks in the forefront of those spiritual luminaries God raised up among the early Methodists. The designated heir to Wesley, not only was he a thoughtful and articulate champion of this great doctrine, he was also, by all contemporary indications, an outstanding example of what he preached and taught. A number of his colleagues and associates testify to his great godliness, remarkable humility and his spiritual passion.

Spend a couple of hours with this saint of God and have your intellect engaged, but even more, let your heart be warmed by his holy fire. You will have taken an important step in being better prepared to give to them who question a sensible and scriptural reason for being a confirmed proponent of Christian perfection as revealed in the Word and enjoyed by multitudes of sanctified pilgrims on their way home.

—DR. MICHAEL R. WILLIAMS
Westfield, In

Preface

CHRISTIAN PERFECTION, ACCORDING TO the account which both Mr. Wesley and Mr. Fletcher have given of it — and consequently in the sense in which the Methodists believe and teach it — is only another name for that "holiness, without which no man shall see the Lord." Hence, every unprejudiced person must allow that it is of the deepest importance to Christian believers, all of whom are called to "go on to perfection," and to "press toward" this "mark for the prize of their high calling of God in Christ Jesus."

But in order that they may do so, it is highly necessary—

1. That Christian perfection be set before them in a clear, distinct and Scriptural point of view.

2. That the way and manner in which they are to go on and press toward this mark of their high calling, so as actually to attain it, be plainly marked out to them.

3. That some suitable directions be given to such as have attained it, to assist them to "stand fast in the" glorious "liberty wherewith Christ hath made them free," to "walk so as to please God," and to let "no man take their crown."

Now all these are done in the following tract, by one whose praise as a writer, as a minister of Jesus Christ, and as a Christian, is in all the churches. He was himself a shining example of Christian perfection.

I once heard him say, in a meeting of religious friends, "It seems to me but a small thing to be saved from all sin. I want to be filled with all the fullness of God." At the same time he expressed an earnest desire that all who were like-minded should wrestle with God in prayer for the fullness of the Spirit, as the hundred and twenty disciples did before the day of Pentecost. He then gave the following lines, with some that precede them:

Come, Holy Ghost, for thee I call;
Spirit of burning come!

> *Refining fire, go through my heart,*
> *Illuminate my soul;*
> *Scatter thy light through every part,*
> *And sanctify the whole.*

After which he said, "The next time I preach, I will preach on the promise of the Spirit," which he did a night or two after with great enlargement from John 7:36-39: "In the last day, that great day of the feast, Jesus stood and cried, saying, if any man thirst, let him come unto me and drink. He that believeth on me, as the Scripture hath said, Out of his belly shall flow rivers of living water. But this spake he of the Spirit, which they that believe on him should receive." And, if I mistake not, the Sunday night following he preached from these words: "The kingdom of heaven suffereth violence, and the violent take if by force" (Matthew 11:12). His word was with such demonstration of the Spirit and power that I felt as if the kingdom of heaven would burst upon us while he was preaching; and all within me cried, "Thy kingdom come! Come, Lord Jesus, come quickly!"

He was the most devoted, the most heavenly, the most Christlike man I ever saw. Like a faithful mirror, he continually received and reflected the image and glory of his Lord. He breathed incessant prayer and praise. He constantly soared above, and yet sat at the feet of everyone. By the indwelling power and fullness of the Holy Ghost his soul was kindled into a flame of Divine love, and did indeed "burn with inextinguishable blaze" for the glory of God and the salvation of his fellow-creatures. All places and all company were alike to him. His constant care and business was to sink and rise deeper and higher into God, and to prevail with all around him to do the same. The more intimately any were acquainted with him, the more cause they saw to affirm that "there was none occasion of stumbling in him."

I am deeply sensible that his worth does not need my insignificant testimony. But his name and his memory to me are like ointment poured forth. I had for several years an uncommon desire to see him, so much that I often involuntarily repeated these words of our Lord to his disciples: "With desire I have desired to eat this Passover with you." With desire I have desired to see Mr. Fletcher; and God fullfilled my desire at a time and in a way which I had not thought of. In August, 1783, at the earnest request of the preachers and the society in Dublin, he and Mrs. Fletcher visited that city. There I had an opportunity of being in company with him almost every day, morning, noon, and night, and of hearing him preach five or six times a week, for near two months. When I consider what a remarkable blessing he was made to me, and the people of that society in general, who received him as an angel of God, I have ever viewed as a striking instance of the Divine condescension and goodness to an unworthy creature. At the recollection of those days—for they were days of the Son of Man!—and of what I and many then heard, and saw, and felt, my heart overflows with gratitude to the Giver of "every good and perfect gift."

I have not made this extract with a view to prevent any from reading the whole of the *Polemical Essay*. By no means. I hope it will have the contrary effect. That excellent treatise is equally calculated to inform the judgment and influence the heart. There the doctrine of Christian perfection is explained at great length, and unanswerably defended. But many of those who see the necessity of Christian perfection, and who earnestly desire to enjoy and walk worthy of it — and to whom therefore the two following addresses are peculiarly needful — have neither time nor inclination (and some of them but little capacity) for reading controversy. Many also can ill afford half a crown or three shillings. Hence, my view in what I have done is to remove these obstacles and to spread as far as possible what, by the blessing of God, is calculated to be extensively useful, and is so necessary to be well understood and carefully attended to by all who desire to "perfect holiness in the fear of God."

In both the addresses there are several quotations (and some of them pretty long) from what Mr. Wesley has written on the subject. So this small tract contains the sentiments and instructions of those two eminent ministers of Jesus Christ, concerning this great work of His Spirit in the soul.

That the Lord may attend it with His blessing, and make it the means of spreading holiness of heart and life, is the earnest prayer of—

—T. RUTHERFORD

Manchester

January 23, 1796

1

Christian Perfection Defined

WE CALL CHRISTIAN PERFECTION the maturity of grace and holiness, which established, adult believers attain to under the Christian dispensation. By this means we distinguish that maturity of grace, both from the ripeness of grace which belongs to the dispensation of the Jews below us, and from the ripeness of glory which belongs to departed saints above us. Hence it appears that, by *Christian perfection*, we mean nothing but the cluster and maturity of the graces which compose the Christian character in the church militant.

In other words, Christian perfection is a spiritual constellation made up of these gracious stars: perfect repentance, perfect faith, perfect humility, perfect meekness, perfect self-denial, perfect resignation, perfect hope, perfect charity for our visible enemies (as well as for our earthly relations) and above all, perfect love for our invisible God, through the explicit knowledge of our Mediator Jesus Christ. As this last star is always accompanied by all the others, as Jupiter is by his satellites, we frequently use (as St. John) the phrase *perfect love* instead of the word *perfection*. We understand by it the pure love of God shed abroad in the heart of established believers by the Holy Ghost, which is abundantly given them under the fullness of the Christian despensation.

2

To Imperfect Believers, Who Cordially Embrace the Doctrine of Christian Perfection

YOUR REGARD FOR SCRIPTURE and reason, and your desire to answer the ends of God's predestination, "by being conformed to the image of his Son," have happily kept or reclaimed you from Antinomianism.

You see the absolute necessity of personally "fulfilling the law of Christ." Your bosom glows with desire to "perfect holiness in the fear of God;" and, far from blushing to be called perfectionists, you openly assert that a perfect faith, productive of perfect love to God and man, is the pearl of great price, for which you are determined to sell all, and which (next to Christ) you will seek early and late, as the one thing needful for your spiritual and eternal welfare. Some directions, therefore, about the manner of seeking this pearl, cannot but be acceptable to you, if they are Scriptural and rational; and such, I humbly trust, are those which follow:

First, if you would attain an evangelically sinless perfection, let your full assent to the truth of that deep doctrine firmly stand upon the evangelical foundation of a precept and a promise. A precept without a promise would not sufficiently animate you; nor would a promise without a precept properly bind you. A Divine precept and a Divine promise form an unshaken foundation. Let then your faith deliberately rest her right foot upon these precepts:

Hear, O Israel—thou shalt love the Lord thy God with all thy heart, and with all thy soul, and with all thy might (Deuteronomy 6:5).

Thou shalt not hate thy neighbour in thy heart; thou shalt in any wise rebuke thy neighbour, and not suffer sin upon him. Thou shalt not avenge, nor bear any grudge against the children of thy people: but thou shalt love thy neighbour as thyself. I am the Lord. Ye shall keep my statutes (Leviticus 19:17, 18).

And now, Israel, what does the Lord thy God require of thee, but to fear the Lord thy God, to walk in his ways, and to love him, and to serve the Lord thy God with all thy heart, and with all thy soul, to keep the commandments of the Lord God, and his statutes, which I command thee this day for thy good...Circumcise therefore the foreskin of your heart, and be no more stiff-necked (Deuteronomy 10:12)

Serve God with a perfect heart, and a willing mind, for the Lord searcheth all hearts, and understandeth the imaginations of the thoughts (1 Chronicles 28:9).

Should unbelief suggest that these are only Old Testament injunctions, trample on that false suggestion, and rest the same foot of your faith upon the following New Testament precepts:

Think not that I am come to destroy the law, or the prophets. I say unto you, Love your enemies; bless them that curse you; do good to them that hate you...that ye may be the children of your Father who is in...For if ye love them which love you, what reward have ye? Do not even the publicans the same? Be ye therefore perfect, even as your Father which is in heaven is perfect (Matthew 5:17, 44)

If thou wilt enter into life, keep the commandments (Matthew 19:17).

Bear ye one another's burdens, and so fulfil the law of Christ (Galatians 6:2).

This is my commandment, that ye love one another as I have loved you (John 15:12).

He that loveth another hath fulfilled the law: for this, Thou shalt not commit adultery...thou shalt not covet, and if there be any other commandment, it is briefly comprehended in this saying, Thou shalt love thy neighbour as thyself. Love worketh no ill," etc., "therefore, love is the fulfilling of the law (Romans 13:8, 10).

This commandment we have from him, that he who loves God, love his brother also (1 John 4:21).

If ye fulfil the royal law, *Thou shalt love thy neighbour as thyself,* ye do well. But if ye have respect to persons, ye commit sin, and are convinced of the law as transgressors (James 2:8,9).

Circumcision is nothing, uncircumcision is nothing [comparatively speaking;] but [under Christ] the keeping of the commandments of God [is the one thing needful]" (1 Corinthians 7:19).

> For the end of the commandment is charity, out of a pure heart, and of a good conscience, and of faith unfeigned (1 Timothy 1:5).

> Though I have all faith...and have not charity, I am nothing (1 Corinthians 13:2).

> Whosoever shall keep the whole law [of liberty] and yet offend in one point [in uncharitable respect of persons] he is guilty of all...So speak ye, and so do, as they that shall be judged by the law of liberty [which requires perfect love, and therefore makes no allowance for the least degree of uncharitableness] (James 2:10, 12).

When the right foot of your faith stands on these evangelical precepts and proclamations, lest she should stagger for lack of a promise adequate in every way for such weighty commandments, let her place her left foot upon the following promises, which are extracted from the Old Testament:

> The Lord thy God will circumcise thine heart, and the heart of thy seed, to love the Lord thy God with all thine heart, and with all thy soul, that thou mayest live (Deuteronomy 30:6).

> Come now, and let us reason together, saith the Lord: though your sins be as scarlet, they shall be as white as snow; though they be red like crimson, they shall be as wool (Isaiah 1:18).

That this promise chiefly refers to sanctification is evident—

1. From the verses which immediately precede it: "Make you clean," etc. "Cease to do evil, learn to do well," etc.

2. From the verses which immediately follow it: "If ye be willing and obedient, ye shall eat the good of the land; but if ye refuse and rebel [or disobey] ye shall be devoured with the sword."

Again:

> I will give them a heart to know me, that I am the Lord, and they shall be my people, and I will be their God, [in a new and peculiar manner] for they shall return unto me with their whole heart. This shall be the covenant that I will make with the house of Israel. After those days, saith the Lord, I will put my law in their inward parts, and write it in their hearts, and will be their God, and they shall be my people (Jeremiah 24:7; 31:33).

> Then will I sprinkle clean water upon you, and ye shall be clean: from all your filthiness and from all your idols, will I cleanse you: a new heart also

will I give you, and a new spirit will I put within you: and I will take away the heart of stone out of your flesh, and I will give you a heart of flesh. And I will put my Spirit within you, and cause you to walk in my statutes, and ye shall keep my judgments and do them (Ezekiel 36:25-27).

Let nobody suppose that the promises of the circumcision of the heart, the cleansing, the clean water, and the Spirit , which are mentioned in these scriptures, and by which the hearts of believers are to be made new, and in which God's law is to be written, that they shall "keep his judgments and do them" — let none, I say, suppose that these glorious promises belong only to the Jews; for their full accomplishment peculiarly refers to the Christian dispensation. Beside, if sprinklings of the Spirit were sufficient, under the Jewish dispensation, to raise the plant of Jewish perfection in Jewish believers, how much more will the revelation of "the horn of our salvation," and the outpourings of the Spirit, raise the plant of Christian perfection in faithful, Christian believers!

This revelation of Christ in the Spirit as well as in the flesh, these emissions of the water of life, these baptisms of fire which burn up the chaff of sin, thoroughly purge God's spiritual floor, save us from all our uncleanness, and deliver us from all our enemies. These blessings, I say, peculiarly promised to Christians, are demonstrated by the following cloud of New Testament declarations and promises:

Blessed be the Lord God of Israel, for he hath raised up a horn of salvation for us, as he spake by the mouth of his holy prophets, that we, being delivered out of the hands of our enemies, might serve him without [unbelieving] fear, [that is, with perfect love] in holiness and righteousness before him all the days of our life (Luke 1:68-75).

Blessed are the poor in spirit, who thirst after righteousness, for they shall be filled (Matthew 5:3, 6).

If thou knewest the gift of God...thou wouldest have asked of him, and he would have given thee living water: and the water that I shall give him, shall be in him a well of water springing up to everlasting life (John 4:10, 14).

Jesus stood and cried, saying, If any man thirst, let him come to me and drink. He that believeth on me, [when I shall have ascended up on high to receive gifts for men] out of his belly shall flow rivers of living water, [to cleanse his soul, and keep it clean.] But this he spake of the Spirit, which they that believe on him should receive; for the Holy Ghost was not yet given, [in such a manner as to raise the plant of Christian perfection] because Jesus was not yet glorified [and his spiritual dispensation was not yet fully opened] (John 7:37) etc.

Mr. Wesley, in his *Plain Account of Christian Perfection,* has published some excellent questions, and proposed them to those who deny perfection to be attainable in this life. They are close to the point and, therefore, the first two attack the imperfectionists from the very ground on which I want you to stand. They say:

1. Has there not been a larger measure of the Holy Spirit given under the Gospel than under the Jewish dispensation? If not, in what sense was the Spirit not given before Christ was glorified? John 7:39.

2. Was that glory which followed the sufferings of Christ (1 Peter 1:11) an external glory, or an internal glory, namely, the glory of holiness?

Always rest the doctrine of Christian perfection on this Scriptural foundation, and it will stand as firm as revelation itself.

It is allowed on all sides that the dispensation of John the Baptist exceeded that of the other prophets, because it immediately introduced the Gospel of Christ, and because John was not only appointed to "preach the baptism of repentance," but also clearly to point out the very person of Christ, and to "give knowledge of salvation to God's people by the remission of sins" (Luke 1:77). Nevertheless, John only promised the blessing of the Spirit, which Christ bestowed when he had received gifts for men. "I indeed," said John, "baptize you with water unto repentance; but he that cometh after me is mightier than I. He shall baptize you with the Holy Ghost and with fire" (Matthew 3:11). Such is the importance of His promise that it is particularly recorded, not only by the three other evangelists (see Mark 1:8; Luke 3:16; and John 1:26) but also by our Lord himself, who said just before his ascension, "John truly baptized with water, but ye shall be baptized with the Holy Ghost not many days hence" (Acts 1:5).

So central is this promise of the Spirit's stronger influences to raise the rare plant of Christian perfection, that when our Lord speaks of this promise, he emphatically calls it *the promise of the Father,* because it shines among the other promises of the Gospel of Christ as the moon does among the stars. Thus, "Wait," says he, "for the promise of the Father, which ye have heard of me" (Acts 1:4). And again, "Behold, I send the promise of my Father upon you" (Luke 24:49).

Agreeing with this, St. Peter says, "Jesus being by the right hand of God exalted, and having received of the Father the promise of the Holy Ghost, he hath shed forth this:" He has begun abundantly to fulfill

> that which was spoken by the Prophet Joel: And it shall come to pass in the last days, saith God, that I will pour out [bestow a more abundant measure] of my Spirit upon all flesh. Therefore repent and be baptized [*i.e.,* make an open profession of your faith] in the name of the Lord Jesus, for the remission of sins; and ye shall receive the gift of the Holy Ghost; for the promise is unto you and to your children, and to as many as the Lord our God shall call [to enjoy the full blessings of the Christian dispensation] (Acts 2:17, 33, 38).

This promise, when it is received in its fullness, is undoubtedly the greatest of all the "exceeding great and precious promises, which are given to us, that by them you might be partakers of the Divine nature [that is, of pure love and unmixed holiness]" (2 Peter 1:4). Have, therefore, a particular look at it, and to these deep words of our Lord:

> I will ask the Father, and he shall give you another Comforter, that he may abide with you for ever, even the Spirit of truth [and power] whom the world knows not…but ye know him, for he remaineth with you, and shall be in you. At that day ye shall know that I am in my Father, and you in me, and I in you: for if any man [*i.e.,* any believer] love me, he will keep my words, and my Father will love him, and we will come to him, and make our abode with him" (John 14:16-17;20, 23).

"Which," says Mr. Wesley in his note on the place, "implies such a large manifestation of the Divine presence and love that the former, in justification, is as nothing compared to it." In agreement with this, the same judicious divine expresses himself thus in another of his publications.

> These virtues [meekness, humility, and true resignation to God] are the only wedding garment; they are the lamps and vessels well furnished with oil. There is nothing that will do instead of them: they must have their full and perfect work in you, or the soul can never be delivered from its fallen, wrathful state. There is no possibility of salvation but in this. And when the Lamb of God has brought forth his own meekness…in our souls, then are our lamps

trimmed, and our virgin hearts made ready for the marriage feast. This marriage feast signifies the entrance into the highest state of union that can be between God and the soul in this life. This birthday of the Spirit of love in our souls, whenever we attain it, will feast our souls with such peace and joy in God, as will blot out the remembrance of every thing that we called peace or joy before.

To make you believe this important promise with more fervor, consider that our Lord spent some of his last moments in sealing it with his powerful intercession. After having prayed the Father to sanctify his disciples through the truth, firmly embraced by their faith, and powerfully applied by his Spirit, he adds, "Neither pray I for these alone, but for them who will believe on me through their word." And what is it that our Lord asks for these believers? Truly, what St. Paul asked for the imperfect believers at Corinth, "even their perfection" (2 Corinthians 13:9).

This is a state of soul which Christ describes:

> That they all may be one, as thou Father art in me, and I in thee, that they may be made one in us…that they may be one as we are one: I in them, and thou in me, that they may be perfected in one, and that the world may know that thou hast loved them as thou hast loved me (John 17:21, 23).

Our Lord could not pray in vain: it is not to be supposed that the Scriptures are silent with respect to the effect of this solemn prayer, an answer to which was to give the world an idea of the New Jerusalem coming down from heaven, a specimen of the power which introduces believers into the state of Christian perfection. Therefore we read that on the day of Pentecost the kingdom of Satan was powerfully shaken, and the kingdom of God, "righteousness, peace, and joy in the Holy Ghost," began to come with a new power. Then were thousands wonderfully converted, and clearly justified; then was the kingdom of heaven taken by force; and the love of Christ and of the brethren began to burn the chaff of selfishness and sin with a force which the world had never seen before. (See Acts 2:42, etc.)

Some time after, another glorious baptism, or primary outpouring of the Spirit, carried the disciples of Christ farther into the kingdom of grace which perfects believers in one. Therefore we find that the account which St. Luke gives of them after this second, cardinal manifestation of the Holy Spirit, in a great degree answers to our

Lord's prayer for their perfection. He had asked "that they all might be one, and that they might be one as the Father and he are one, and that they might be perfected in one" (John 17:21, 13).

Now a fuller answer is given to his deep request. Take it in the words of the inspired historian:

> And when they had prayed, the place was shaken where they were assembled together, and they were [once more] filled with the Holy Ghost, and they spake the word with [still greater] boldness; and the multitude of them that believed were of one heart, and of one soul; neither said any of them, that aught of the things which he possessed were his own; but they had all things common…and great grace was upon them all (Acts 4:31-33)!

Who does not see in this account a specimen of that grace which our Lord had asked for believers, when he had prayed that his disciples, and those who would believe on him through their word, might be "perfected in one?"

It may be asked here, whether "the multitude of them that believed" in those happy days were all perfect in love? I answer, that if pure love had cast out all selfishness, and sinful fear from their hearts, they were undoubtedly "made perfect in love." But as God does not usually remove the plague of indwelling sin till it has been discovered and lamented, and as we find in the two next chapters an account of the guile of Ananias and his wife, and of the partiality or selfish murmuring of some believers, it seems that those chiefly, who before were strong in the grace of their dispensation, arose then into sinless fathers. The first love of other believers, through the peculiar blessing of Christ upon his infant Church, was so bright and powerful for a time that little children had, or seemed to have, the strength of young men, and young men the grace of fathers.

In this case, the account which St. Luke gives of the primitive believers ought to be taken with some restriction. Thus, while many of them were perfect in love, many might have the imperfection of their love only covered over by a land flood of peace and joy in believing. And, in this case, what is said of their being "all of one heart and mind, and of their having all things common," etc., may only mean that the harmony of love had not yet been broken, and that none had yet betrayed any of the uncharitableness for which Christians in after ages became so conspicuous.

With respect to the "great grace which was upon them all," this does not necessarily mean that they were all equally strong in grace; for great unity and happiness may rest upon a whole family where the difference between a father, a young man, and a child, continues to subsist. However, it is not improbable that God, to open the dispensation of the Spirit, in a manner which might fix the attention of all ages upon its importance and glory, permitted the whole body of believers to take an extraordinary turn together into the Canaan of perfect love, and to show the world the admirable fruit which grows there, as the spies sent by Joshua took a turn into the good land of promise before they were settled in it, and brought from thence the bunch of grapes which astonished and encouraged the Israelites, who had not yet crossed Jordan.

Upon the whole it is, I think, undeniable, from the four first chapters of the Acts, that a peculiar power of the Spirit is bestowed upon believers under the Gospel of Christ. This power, through faith on our part, can operate the most sudden and surprising change in our souls. When our faith shall fully embrace the promise of full sanctification, or of a complete "circumcision of the heart in the Spirit," the Holy Ghost, who kindled so much love on the day of Pentecost that all the primitive believers loved or seemed to love each other perfectly, will not fail to help us to love one another without sinful self seeking. As soon as we do so, "God dwelleth in us, and his love is perfected in us" (1 John 4:12; John 14:23).

Should you ask, how many baptisms, or effusions of the sanctifying Spirit are necessary to cleanse a believer from all sin, and to kindle his soul into perfect love; I reply, The effect of a sanctifying truth depends upon the ardor of the faith with which that truth is embraced, and upon the power of the Spirit with which it is applied. I should betray a want of modesty if I brought the operations of the Holy Ghost, and the energy of faith, under a rule which is not expressly laid down in the Scriptures. If you ask your physician how many doses of medicine you must take before all the crudities of your stomach can be carried off, and your appetite perfectly restored, he would probably answer you that this depends upon the nature of those crudities, the strength of the medicine, and the manner in which your constitution will allow it to operate. In general you must repeat the dose, as you can bear, till the remedy has fully answered the desired end.

I return a similar answer. If one powerful baptism of the Spirit "seal you unto the day of redemption, and cleanse you from all [moral] filthiness," so much the better. If two or more be necessary, the Lord can repeat them. "His arm is not shortened, that it cannot save;" nor is his promise of the Spirit stinted. He says, in general,

> Whosoever will, let him come and take of the water of life freely. If you, being evil, know how to give good gifts unto your children, how much more will your heavenly Father [who is goodness itself] give his Holy [sanctifying] Spirit to them that ask him!

I may, however, venture to say, in general, that before we can rank among perfect Christians, we must receive so much of the truth and Spirit of Christ by faith, as to have the pure love of God and man shed abroad in our hearts by the Holy Ghost given unto us, and to be filled with the meek and lowly mind which was in Christ. If one outpouring of the Spirit, one bright manifestation of the sanctifying truth, so empties us of self as to fill us with the mind of Christ and with pure love, we are undoubtedly Christians in the full sense of the word. From the ground of my soul I, therefore, subscribe to the answer which a great divine makes to the following objection: "But some who are newly justified, do come up to this [Christian perfection:] what then will you say to these?" Mr. Wesley says with great propriety,

> If they really do, I will say, they are sanctified, saved from sin *in that moment;* and that they never need lose what God has given, or feel sin any more. But certainly this is an unusual case. It is otherwise with the generality of those that are justified. They feel in themselves, more or less, pride, anger, self-will, and a heart bent to backsliding. And till they have *gradually* mortified these, they are not fully renewed in love. God usually gives a considerable time for men to receive light, to grow in grace, to do and to suffer his will before they are either justified or sanctified. But he does not invariably adhere to this. Sometimes he "cuts short his work." He does the work of many years in a few weeks; perhaps in a week, a day, an hour. He justifies, or sanctifies both those who have done or suffered nothing, and who have not had time for a gradual growth either in light or grace. And may he not "do what he will with his own? Is thine eye evil, because he is good?" It need not therefore

be proved by forty texts of Scripture, either that most men are perfected in love *at last,* or that there is a gradual work of God in the soul; and that, generally speaking, it is *a long time,* even many years, before sin is destroyed. All this we know. But we know, likewise, that God may, with man's good leave, "cut short his work" in whatever degree he pleases, and do the usual work of many years in a moment. He does so in a great many instances. And yet there is a gradual work both before and after that moment. So that one may affirm, the work is *gradual;* another, it is *instantaneous,* without any manner of contradiction. (*Plain Account,* page 115, etc.)

On page 155, the same eminent divine explains himself more fully:

It [Christian perfection] is constantly preceded and followed by a *gradual* work. But is it in itself *instantaneous* or not? In examining this, let us go on step by step. An instantaneous change has been wrought in some believers. None can deny this. Since that change, they enjoy perfect love. They feel this, and this alone. They "rejoice evermore, pray without ceasing, in every thing give thanks." Now this is all that I mean by *perfection.* Therefore these are witnesses of the perfection which I preach.

"But in some this change was not instantaneous." They did not perceive the instant when it was wrought. It is often difficult to perceive the instant when a man dies. Yet there is an instant in which life ceases. And if ever sin ceases, there must be a last moment of its existence, and a first moment of our deliverance from it.

"But if they have this love now, they will lose it." They may, but they need not. And whether they do or not, they have it now. They now experience what we teach. They now are *all love.* They now rejoice, pray, and praise without ceasing.

"However, sin is only suspended in them; it is not destroyed." Call it which you please. They are all love to-day and they take no thought for the morrow.

To return: When you firmly assent to the truth of the precepts and promises, on which the doctrine of Christian perfection is founded; when you understand the meaning of these scriptures: "Sanctify them through thy truth, thy word is truth; I will send the Comforter [the Spirit of truth and holiness] unto you; God hath chosen you to [eternal] salvation through sanctification of the Spirit and belief of the truth:" when you see that the way to Christian perfection is by the word of the Gospel of Christ, by faith, and by the Spirit of God; in the next place, get tolerably clear ideas of this perfection.

This is absolutely necessary. If you will hit a mark, you must know where it is. Some people aim at Christian perfection, but mistaking it for angelical perfection, they shoot above the mark, miss it, and then peevishly give up their hopes. Others place the mark much too low; hence you hear them profess to have attained Christian perfection when they have not so much as attained the mental serenity of a philosopher, or the candor of a good-natured, conscientious heathen.

In the preceding pages, if I am not mistaken, the mark is fixed according to the rules of Scriptural moderation. It is not placed so high as to make you despair of hitting it, if you do your best in an evangelical manner; nor yet so low as to allow you to presume that you can reach it without exerting all your abilities to the uttermost, in due subordination to the efficacy of Jesus' blood, and the Spirit's sanctifying influences.

Should you ask, "Which is the way to Christian perfection? Shall we go on to it by internal stillness, in agreement with the direction of Moses and David? 'The Lord will fight for you, and ye shall hold your peace; stand still and see the salvation of God. Be still and know that I am God. Stand in awe and sin not; commune with your own heart upon your bed, and be still.' Or shall we press after it by an internal wrestling, according to these commands of Christ? 'Strive to enter in at the strait gate: the kingdom of heaven suffereth violence, and the violent take it by force.'" etc. According to the evangelical balance of the doctrines of free grace and free will, I answer that the way to perfection is by the due combination of prevenient, assisting free grace, and of submissive, assisted free will.

Antinomian stillness, therefore, which says that free grace must do all, is not the way. Pharisaic activity, which will do most, if not all, is not the way. Join these two partial systems, allowing free grace the lead and high pre-eminence which it so justly claims, and you have the balance of the two Gospel axioms. You do justice to the doctrines of mercy and justice on the one hand, and of free grace and free will on the other; of Divine faithfulness in keeping the covenant of grace, and of human faithfulness in laying hold on that covenant, and keeping within its bounds: in short, you have the Scriptural method of waiting upon God, which Mr. Wesley describes thus:

Restless, resign'd, for God I wait,
  For God my vehement soul stands still.

To understand these lines, consider that faith — like the Virgin Mary — is alternately a receiver and a bestower. First, it passively receives the impregnation of Divine grace, saying, "Behold the handmaid of the Lord: let it be done to me according to thy word," and then it actively brings forth its heavenly fruit with earnest labor. "God worketh in you to will and to do," says St. Paul. Here he describes the passive office of faith, which submits to and acquiesces in every dispensation and operation. "Therefore work out your salvation with fear and trembling," (and, of consequence, with haste, diligence, ardor, and faithfulness). Here the apostle describes the active office of that mother grace, which carefully lays out the talent she has already received.

Would you then wait aright for Christian perfection? Impartially admit both Gospel axioms, and faithfully reduce them to practice. In order to accomplish this, let them meet in your hearts, as the two legs of a pair of compasses meet in the rivet, which makes them one compounded instrument. Let your faith in the doctrine of free grace and Christ's righteousness fix your mind upon God as you fix one of the legs of your compass immovably in the center of the circle which you are about to draw. So shall you "stand still," according to the first text produced in the question. Then let your faith in the doctrine of free will, and evangelical obedience, make you steadily run the circle of duty round that firm center. So shall you imitate the other leg of the compass, which evenly moves around the center, and traces the circumference of a perfect circle.

By this activity, subordinate to grace, you will "take the kingdom of heaven by force." When your heart quietly rests in God, by faith, as it steadily acts the part of a passive receiver, it resembles the leg of the compass which rests in the center of the circle. Then the poet's expressions, "restful—resigned," describe its fixedness in God. But when your heart swiftly moves toward God by faith, as it acts the part of a diligent worker, when your ardent soul follows after God as a thirsty deer does after the water brooks, it may be compared to the leg of the compasses which traces the circumference of the circle; and then these words of the poet, "restless and vehement," properly belong to it. To go on steadily to perfection, you must therefore endeavor steadily to believe, according to the doctrine of the first Gospel axiom, and (as there is opportunity) diligently to work, according to the doctrine of the second. The moment your faith is steadily fixed in God as in your center, and your obedience swiftly moves in the circle of duty from the rest and power which you find in that center you have attained, you are made perfect in the faith which works by love. Your humble faith saves you from Pharisaism, your obedient love from Antinomianism, and both, in due subordination to Christ, constitute you a just man made perfect according to your dispensation.

Another question has also puzzled many sincere perfectionists, and the solution of it may remove a considerable hindrance out of your way: "Is Christian perfection," say they, "to be *instantaneously* brought down to us, or are we *gradually* to grow up to it? Shall we be made perfect in love by a habit of holiness suddenly infused into us, or by acts of feeble faith and feeble love so frequently repeated as to become strong, habitual, and evangelically natural to us, according to the well-known maxim, 'A strong habit is a second nature?'"

Both ways are good; and instances of some believers *gradually* perfected, and of others [comparatively speaking] *instantaneously* fixed in perfect love, might probably be produced if we were acquainted with the experiences of all those who have died in a state of evangelical perfection. It may be with the root of sin, as it is with its fruit: some souls parley many years before they can be persuaded to give up all their outward sins, and others part with them, as it were, instantaneously. You may compare the former to those besieged towns which make a long resistance, or to those mothers who go through a tedious and lingering labor. The latter resemble those fortresses which are surprised and carried by storm, or those women who are delivered almost as soon as labor comes upon them.

Travelers inform us that vegetation is so quick and powerful in some warm climates, that the seeds of some vegetables yield a salad in less than twenty-four hours. Should a northern philosopher say, "Impossible!" and should an English gardener exclaim against such *mushroom salad,* they would only expose their prejudices, as do those who decry instantaneous justification, or mock at the possibility of the instantaneous destruction of indwelling sin.

For where is the absurdity of this doctrine? If the light of a candle brought into a dark room can instantly expel the darkness; and if, upon opening your shutters at noon, your gloomy apartment can instantaneously be filled with bright sunlight, why may not the instantaneous rending of the veil of unbelief, or the sudden and full opening of the eye of faith, instantly fill your soul with the light of truth, and the fire of love; supposing the Sun of righteousness arise upon you with powerful healing in his wings? May not the Sanctifier descend upon your waiting soul as quickly as the Spirit descended upon your Lord at his baptism? Did it not descend "as a dove," that is, with the soft motion of a dove, which swiftly shoots down, and instantly lights?

A good man said once, with truth, "A speck is little when it is compared with the sun; but I am far less before God." Alluding to this comparison, I ask, If the sun could instantly kindle a speck — no, if a burning glass can in a moment calcify a bone, and turn a stone to lime — and if the dim flame of a candle can in the twinkling of an eye destroy the flying insect which comes within its sphere, how unscriptural and irrational is it to suppose that, when God fully baptizes a soul with his sanctifying Spirit and with the celestial fire of his love, he cannot in an instant destroy the man of sin, burn up the chaff of corruption, melt the heart of stone into a heart of flesh, and kindle the believing soul into pure, seraphic love!

An appeal to parallel cases may throw some light upon the question which I answer. If you were sick, and asked of God the perfect recovery of your health, how would you look for it? Would you expect to have your strength restored to you at *once,* without any external means, as the lepers who were instantly cleansed; and as the paralytic who, at our Lord's word, took up the bed upon which he lay, and carried it away upon his shoulders? Or by using some external means of a slower operation, as the "ten lepers" did, who were more "gradually cleansed as they went to show themselves to the priests?" Or as King Hezekiah, whose gradual, but equally sure recovery, was owing to God's blessing upon the poultice of figs prescribed by Isaiah? Again, if you were blind, and besought the Lord to give you perfect human sight, how should you wait for it? As Bartimeus, whose eyes were opened in an instant? Or as the man who received his sight by degrees? At first he saw nothing. By and by he confusedly discovered the objects before him, but at last he saw all things clearly. Would you not earnestly wait for an answer to your prayers now, leaving to Divine wisdom the particular manner of your recovery?

Why should you not go and do likewise with respect to the dreadful disorder which we call *indwelling sin?* If our hearts be purified by faith, as the Scriptures expressly testify; if the faith which peculiarly purifies the hearts of Christians be a faith in "the promise of the Father," which promise was made by the Son and directly points at a peculiar effusion of the Holy Ghost, the purifier of spirits; if we may believe in a moment; and if God may, in a moment, seal our sanctifying faith by sending us a fullness of his sanctifying Spirit: if this, I say, be the case, does it not follow, that to deny the possibility of the instantaneous destruction of sin, is to deny, contrary to Scripture and matter of fact, that we can make an instantaneous act of faith in the sanctifying promise of the Father, and in the all-cleansing blood of the Son, and that God can seal that act by the instantaneous operation of his Spirit? This is that which St. Paul calls the *"circumcision* of the heart in [or by] the Spirit," according to the Lord's ancient promise, "I will circumcise thy heart, to love the Lord thy God with all thy heart." Where is the absurdity of believing that "the God of all grace" can give an answer to the poet's rational and evangelical request?

> *Open my faith's interior eye;*
> *Display thy glory from above:*
> *And sinful self shall sink and die,*
> *Lost in astonishment and love.*

If a momentary display of Christ's bodily glory could in an instant turn Saul, the blaspheming, bloody persecutor, into Paul, the praying, gentle apostle; if a sudden sight of Christ's hands could, in a moment, root up from Thomas' heart that detestable resolution, "I will not believe," and produce that deep confession of faith, "My Lord and my God!" what cannot the display of Christ's spiritual glory operate in a believing soul, to which he manifests himself "according to that power whereby he is able to subdue all things to himself?"

Again: if Christ's body could, in an instant, become so glorious on the mount that his very garments partook of the sudden irradiation, became not only free from every spot, but also "white as the light, shining exceeding white as snow, so as no fuller on earth could whiten them;" and if our bodies "shall be changed, if this corruptible shall put on incorruption, and if this mortal shall put on immortality, in a moment, in the twinkling of an eye, at the last trump;" why may not our believing souls, when they fully submit to God's terms, be fully changed—fully turned from the power of Satan unto God? When the Holy Ghost says, "Now is the day of salvation," does he exclude salvation from heart iniquity?

If Christ now deserves fully the *name* of JESUS, "because he *fully* saves his believing people from their sins;" and if now the Gospel trumpet sounds, and sinners arise from the dead, why should we not, upon the performance of the condition, be changed in a moment from indwelling sin to indwelling holiness? Why should we not pass, in the twinkling of an eye, or in a short time, from indwelling death to indwelling life?

This is not all. If you deny the possibility of a quick destruction of indwelling sin, you send to hell — or to some unscriptural purgatory — not only the dying thief but also all those martyrs who suddenly embraced the Christian faith, and were instantly put to death by bloody persecutors for confessing the faith which they had just embraced. If you allow that God may "cut his work short in righteousness" in such case, why not in other cases? Why not, especially when a believer confesses his indwelling sin, fervently prays Christ will, and sincerely believes that Christ can, "now cleanse him from all unrighteousness?"

Nobody is so apt to laugh at the instantaneous destruction of sin as the Calvinists, and yet (such is the inconsistency which characterizes some men!) their doctrine of purgatory is built upon it. For, if you credit them, all dying believers have a nature which is still morally corrupted, and a heart which is yet desperately wicked. These believers, still full of indwelling sin, instantaneously breathe out their last and, without any special act of faith, without any unusual outpouring of the sanctifying Spirit, corruption is instantaneously gone. The indwelling "man of sin" has passed through the Geneva purgatory. He is entirely consumed! And behold! the souls which would not hear of the instantaneous act of a sanctifying faith — which receives the indwelling Spirit of holiness — the souls which pleaded hard for the continuance of indwelling sin are now completely sinless. In the twinkling of an eye they appear in the third heaven among the spirits of just Christians made perfect in love! Such is the doctrine of our opponents. Yet they think it incredible that God should do for us, while we pray in faith, what they suppose death will do for them when they lie in his cold arms, perhaps delirious or senseless!

On the other hand, to deny that imperfect believers may and do gradually grow in grace, and of course that the remains of their sins may and do gradually decay, is as absurd as to deny that God waters the earth by daily dews, as well as by thundershowers. It is as ridiculous as to assert that nobody is carried off by lingering disorders, but that all men die suddenly or a few hours after they are taken ill. I use these comparisons about death to throw some light upon the question which I solve, and not to insinuate that the decay and destruction of sin run parallel with the decay and dissolution of the body, and that of course sin must end with our bodily life. Were I to admit this unscriptural tenet, I should build again what I have all along endeavored to destroy, and as I love consistency, I should promise eternal salvation to all unbelievers; for unbelievers, I presume, will die, *i.e.,* will go into the Geneva purgatory, as well as believers. Nor do I see why death should not be able to destroy the *van* and the *main body* of sin's forces, if it can so readily cut the *rear* (the remains of sin) in pieces.

From the preceding observations, it appears that believers generally go on to Christian perfection, as the disciples went to the other side of the Sea of Galilee. They toiled some time very hard, and with little success. But after they had

rowed about twenty-five or thirty furlongs, they saw Jesus walking on the sea. He said to them, *It is I, be not afraid:* then they willingly received him into the ship, and immediately the ship was at the land whither they went.

Just so, we toil till our faith discovers Christ in the promise, and welcomes him into our hearts. Such is the effect of his presence that immediately we arrive at the land of perfection. Or, to use another illustration, God says to believers, "Go to the Canaan of perfect love: arise, why do ye tarry? Wash away the remains of sin, calling, *i.e.,* believing, on the name of the Lord." And if they submit to the obedience of faith, he deals with them as he did with the Evangelist Philip, to whom he had said, "Arise and go toward the south." For when they "arise and run," as Philip did, "the Spirit of the Lord takes" them, as he did the evangelist, and they are found in the New Jerusalem, as "Philip was found at Azotus." They "dwell in God, [or in perfect love] and God [or perfect love] dwells in them."

Hence it follows that the most evangelical method of following after the perfection to which we are immediately called, is that of seeking it *now,* by endeavoring *fully* to lay hold on the promise of that perfection through faith, just as if our repeated acts of obedience could never help us forward. But, in the meantime, we should do the works of faith, and repeat our internal and external acts of obedience with as much earnestness and faithfulness, according to our present power, as if we were sure to enter into rest merely by a diligent use of our talents, and a faithful exertion of the powers which Divine grace has bestowed upon us. If we do not attend to the first of these directions, we shall seek to be sanctified by works like the Pharisees. If we disregard the second, we shall fall into the sin of Solifidian sloth with the Antinomians.

This double direction is founded upon the connection of the two Gospel axioms. If the second axiom, which implies the doctrine of free will, were false, I would only say, "Be still, or rather do nothing. Free grace alone will do all in you and for you." But as this axiom is as true as the first, I must add, "Strive in humble subordination to free grace. For Christ saith, 'To him that hath' initiating grace to purpose, 'more grace shall be given, and he shall have abundance.' His faithful and equitable Benefactor will give him the reward of perfecting grace."

Beware, therefore, of unscriptural refinements. Set out for the Canaan of perfect love with a firm resolution to labor for the rest which remains on earth for the people of God. Some good, mistaken men, wise above what is written, and fond of striking out on paths which were unknown to the apostles — new paths marked out by voluntary humility, and leading to Antinomianism — some people of that stamp, I say, have made it their business, from the days of heated Augustine, to decry making resolutions. They represent this practice as a branch of what they are pleased to call *legality*. They insinuate that it is utterly inconsistent with the knowledge of our inconstancy and weakness. In a word, they frighten us from the first step to Christian perfection; from an humble evangelical determination to run till we reach the prize or, if you please, to go down till we come to the lowest place.

It may not be amiss to point out the ground of their mistake. Once they broke the balance of the Gospel axioms by leaning too much toward free will, and by not laying their first and principal stress upon free grace, God, to bring them to the evangelical mean, refused his blessing on their unevangelical willing and running. Hence it is that their self-righteous resolutions started aside like a broken bow. When they found out their mistake, instead of coming back to the line of moderation, they fled to the other extreme. Casting all their weights into the scale of free grace, they absurdly formed a resolution never to form a resolution. Determining not to throw one determination into the scale of free will, they began to draw all the believers they met with into the ditch of a slothful quietism and Laodicean stillness.

You will never steadily go on to perfection unless you get over this mistake. Let the imperfectionists laugh at you for making humble resolutions. Go on "steadfastly purposing to lead a new life," as says our Church and in order to this, "steadfastly purpose" to get *a new heart* in the full sense of the word. So long as your heart continues partly *unrenewed,* your life will be partly *unholy.* Therefore, St. James justly observes that "if any man offend not in word, he is a perfect man," he loves God with all his heart, his heart is fully renewed; it being impossible that a heart still tainted in part with vanity and guile should always dictate the words of sincerity and love. Your good resolutions need not fail, nor will they fail if, under a due sense of the fickleness and helplessness of your unassisted free will, you properly depend upon God's faithfulness and *assistance.* However, should they fail, as they probably will do more than once, be not discouraged but repent. Search out the cause and, in the strength of free grace, let your assisted free will renew your evangelical purpose till the Lord seals it with his mighty *fiat,* and says, "Let it be done to thee according to thy resolving faith."

It is much better to be laughed at as "poor creatures, who know nothing of themselves," than to be deluded as foolish virgins who fondly imagine that their vessels are full of imputed oil. Take therefore the sword of the Spirit and boldly cut this dangerous snare in pieces. Conscious of your impotence and yet laying out your talent of free will, say with the prodigal son, "I will arise and go to my father." Say with David,

> I will love thee, O Lord my God: I will behold thy face in righteousness: I am purposed that my mouth shall not transgress: I will keep it, as it were, with a bridle: I have said that I would keep thy word: the proud, [and they who are humble in an unscriptural way] have had me exceedingly in derision, but I will keep thy precepts with my whole heart. I have sworn, and I will perform it, that I will keep thy righteous judgments.

Say with St. Paul, "I am determined not to know anything save Jesus, and him crucified." And with Jacob, "I will not let thee go, unless thou bless me*!*" To sum up all good resolutions in one, if you are a member of the Church of England, say, "I have engaged to renounce all the vanities of this wicked world, all the sinful lusts of the flesh, and all the works of the devil: to believe all the articles of the Christian faith; and to keep God's commandments all the days of my life." That is, I have most solemnly resolved to be a perfect Christian. And this resolution I have publicly sealed by receiving the two sacraments upon it: baptism, after my parents and sponsors had laid me under this blessed vow, and the Lord's Supper, after I had personally ratified, in the bishop's presence, what they had done. Nor do I only think that I am bound to keep this vow; but

> by God's grace so I will; and I heartily thank our heavenly Father, that he has called me to this state of salvation [and Christian perfection;] and I pray unto him to give me his grace, that I may not only attain it, but also continue in the same unto my life's end. (*Church Catechism*)

"Much diligence," says Kempis, "is necessary to him that will profit much. If he who firmly purposes often fails, what shall he do who seldom or feebly purposes anything?" But I say it again and again, do not lean upon your free will and good purposes, so as to encroach upon the glorious preeminence of free grace. Let the first gospel axiom stand invariably in its honorable place. Lay your principal stress upon Divine mercy and say with the good man, whom I have just quoted, "Help me, O Lord God, in your holy service, and grant that I may now this day begin perfectly." In following this method, you will do the two Gospel axioms justice. You will so depend upon God's free grace as not to fall into Pharisaic running, and you will so exert your own free will as not to slide into Antinomian sloth. Your course lies exactly between these rocks. To pass these perilous straits, your resolving heart must acquire a heavenly polarity. Through the spiritually magnetic touch of Christ, the cornerstone, your soul must learn to point toward faith and works, or if you please, toward a due submission to free grace, and a due exertion of free will, as the opposite ends of the needle of a compass point toward the north and the south.

From this direction flows the following advice. Resolve to be perfect *in* yourselves, but not *of* yourselves: the Antinomians boast that they are perfect only in their heavenly representative. Christ was filled with perfect humility and love: they are perfect in his person. They need not a perfection of humble love in themselves. To avoid their error, be perfect in yourselves and not in another. Let your perfection of humility and love be inherent. Let it dwell in you. Let it fill your own heart and influence your own life. So shall you avoid the delusions of the virgins, who give you to understand that the oil of their perfection is all contained in the sacred vessel which formerly hung on the cross, and therefore their salvation is finished. They have oil enough in that rich vessel, manna enough and to spare in that golden pot. Christ's heart was perfect, and therefore theirs may safely remain imperfect, yes, full of indwelling sin, till death, the messenger of the bridegroom, comes to cleanse them and fill them with perfect love at the midnight cry!

Delusive hope! Can anything be more absurd than for a sapless, dry branch to fancy that it has sap and moisture enough in the vine which it cumbers? or for an impenitent adulterer to boast that "in the Lord he has" chastity and righteousness? Where did Christ ever say, "Have salt in another?" Does he not say, Take heed, that ye be not deceived! Have salt in "yourselves" (Mark 9:50)? Does he not impute the destruction of stony ground hearers to their "not having root in themselves" (Matthew 13:21)?

If it was the patient man's comfort, that "the root of the matter was found in him," is it not deplorable to hear modern believers say, without any explanatory clause, that they have nothing but sin in themselves? But is it enough to have *"the root* in ourselves?" Must we not also have *the fruit,* yes, "be filled with the fruits of righteousness"(Philippians 1:11)? Is it not St. Peter's doctrine, where he says, "If these things be in you, and abound, ye shall neither be barren nor unfruitful in the knowledge of Christ"(2 Peter 1:8)? And is it not that of David, where he prays, "Create in me a clean heart," etc?

Away, then, with all Antinomian refinements! And if with St. Paul you will have salvation and rejoicing in yourselves and not in another, make sure of holiness and perfection "in yourselves, and not in another."

But while you endeavor to avoid the snare of the Antinomians, do not run into that of the Pharisees, who will have their perfection *of themselves* and therefore, by their own unevangelical efforts, self-concerted willings, and self-prescribed runnings, they endeavor to "raise sparks of their own kindling, and to warm themselves" by their own painted fires and fruitless agitations. Feel your impotence. Own that "no man has quickened [and perfected] his own soul." Be content to invite, receive, and welcome the light of life, but never attempt to form or to control it. It is your duty to wait for the morning light, and to rejoice when it visits you, but if you grow so self-conceited as to say, "I will create a sun: *let there be light,*" or if, when the light visits your eyes you say, "I will accumulate a stock of light. I will so fill my eyes with light today, that tomorrow I shall be almost able to do my work without the sun, or at least without a constant dependence upon its beams," would you not betray a species of self-deifying idolatry and Satanical pride?

If our Lord himself, as "Son of man," would not have one grain of human goodness himself; if he said, "Why callest thou me *good?* There is none good [*self-good,* or *good of himself*] but God;" who can wonder enough at those proud Christians who claim some self-originated goodness, boasting of what they have received as if they had not received it, or using what they have received without an humble sense of their constant dependence upon their heavenly Benefactor. To avoid this horrid delusion of the Pharisees learn to see, to feel, and to acknowledge, that of the Father, through the Son, and by the Holy Ghost, are all your urim and thummim, *your lights and perfections.* And while the Lord says, "From me is thy fruit found" (Hosea 14:8) bow at his footstool and gratefully reply, "Of thy fullness have all we received, and grace for grace"(John 1:16). For thou art "the Father of lights, from whom cometh every good and perfect gift" (James 1:17). "Of thee, and through thee, and to thee are all things: to thee [therefore] be the glory for ever. *Amen.*" (Romans 11:36).

You will have this humble and thankful disposition if you let your repentance cast deeper roots. For if Christian perfection implies a forsaking of all inward as well as outward sin; and if true repentance is a grace *whereby we forsake sin,* it follows that to attain Christian perfection, we must so follow our Lord's evangelical precept — "Repent, for the kingdom of heaven is at hand" — as to leave no sin, no bosom sin, no indwelling sin *unrepented of,* and of consequence, *unforsaken.* He whose heart is still full of indwelling sin has no more truly repented of indwelling sin than the man whose mouth is still defiled with filthy talking and jesting has truly repented of his crude and indecent language. The deeper our sorrow for, and detestation of indwelling sin is, the more penitently do we confess the plague of our hearts; and when we properly confess it, we inherit the blessing promised in these words: "If we confess our sins, he is faithful and just to forgive us our sins, and to cleanse us from all unrighteousness" (I John 1:9).

To promote this deep repentance, consider how many spiritual evils still haunt your breast. Look into the inward "chamber of imagery," where assuming self-love, surrounded by a multitude of vain thoughts, foolish desires, and wild imaginations, keeps her court. Grieve that your heart, which should be all flesh, is yet partly stone; and that your soul, which should be only a temple for the Holy Ghost, is yet so frequently turned into a den of thieves, a hole for the cockatrice, a nest for a brood of spiritual vipers, for the remains of envy, jealousy, fretfulness, anger, pride, impatience, peevishness, formality, sloth, prejudice, bigotry, carnal confidence, evil shame, self righteousness, tormenting fears, uncharitable suspicions, idolatrous love, and I know not how many of the evils which form the retinue of hypocrisy and unbelief.

Through grace detect these evils by a close attention to what passes in your own heart at all times, but especially in an hour of temptation. By frequent and deep confession, drag out all these abominations, these sins, which would not have Christ to reign alone over you, bring before him. Place them in the light of his countenance. If you do it in faith, that light and the warmth of his love will kill them as the light and heat of the sun kill the worms which the plow turns up to the open air on a dry summer's day.

Nor plead that you can do nothing, for by the help of Christ, who is always ready to assist the helpless, you can solemnly say upon your knees what you have probably said in an airy manner to your professing friends. If you ever acknowledged to them that your heart is deceitful, prone to leave undone what you ought to do, and ready to do what you ought to leave undone, you can undoubtedly make the same confession to God. Complain to him who can help you as you have done to those who cannot. Lament, as you are able, the darkness of your mind, the stubbornness of your will, the dullness or exorbitancy of your affections, and persistently entreat the God of all grace to "renew a right spirit

within" you. If you "sorrow after this godly sort, what carefulness will
be "wrought in you! what indignation! what fear! what vehement desire!
what zeal! yea, what revenge!" You will then sing in faith, what the
imperfectionists sing in unbelief:

> *O how I hate those lusts of mine,*
> *That crucified my God:*
> *Those sins that pierced and nail'd his flesh*
> *Fast to the fatal wood!*
>
> *Yes, my Redeemer, they shall die,*
> *My heart hath so decreed;*
> *Nor will I spare those guilty things*
> *That made my Saviour bleed.*
> *While with a melting, broken heart,*
> *My murder'd Lord I view,*
> *I'll raise revenge against my sins,*
> *And slay the murderers too.*

Closely connected with this deep repentance is the practice of a
judicious, universal self-denial. "If thou wilt be perfect," says our Lord,

deny thyself, take up thy cross daily, and follow me. He that loveth father or
mother [much more he that loveth praise, pleasure, or money] more than me,
is not worthy of me: [nay,] Whosoever will save his life shall lose it; and
whosoever will lose it for my sake, shall find it.

Many desire to live and reign with Christ, but few choose to suffer
and die with him. However, as the way of the cross leads to heaven, it
undoubtedly leads to Christian perfection. To avoid the cross, therefore,
or to decline drinking the cup of vinegar and gall which God permits
your friends or foes to mix for you, is to throw away the aloes which
Divine wisdom puts to the breasts of the mother of harlots, to wean you
from her and her witchcrafts. It is to refuse a medicine which is kindly
prepared to restore your health and appetite. In a word, it is to renounce
the Physician who "heals all our infirmities," when we take his bitter
draughts, submit to have our abscess opened by his sharp scalpel, and
yield to have our proud flesh wasted away by his painful caustics.

Our Lord "was made a perfect *Savior* through sufferings," and we may be made perfect Christians in the same manner. We may be called to suffer till all that which we have brought out of spiritual Egypt is consumed in a howling wilderness, in a dismal Gethsemane, or on a shameful Calvary. Should this lot be reserved for us, let us not imitate our Lord's imperfect disciples, who "forsook him and fled," but let us stand the fiery trial till all our fetters are melted and our dross is purged away.

Fire is of a purgative nature. It separates the dross from the gold, and the fiercer it is, the more quick and powerful is its operation.

> He that is left in Zion, and he that remaineth in Jerusalem, shall be called holy... when the Lord shall have washed away the filth of the daughters of Zion, and shall have purged the blood of Jerusalem by the spirit of judgment and by the spirit of burning (Isaiah 4:4).

> I will bring the third part through the fire, saith the Lord, and will refine them as silver is refined, and will try them as gold is tried; they shall call on my name, and I will hear them: I will say, It is my people; and they shall say, The Lord is my God (Zechariah 13:9).

Therefore, if the Lord should allow the best men in his camp, or the strongest men in Satan's army, to cast you into a furnace of fiery temptations, come not out of it till you are called. "Let patience have its perfect work." Meekly keep your trying station till your heart is disengaged from all that is earthly, and till the sense of God's preserving power kindles in you such a faith in his omnipotent love as few experimentally know but they who have seen themselves, like the mysterious bush in Horeb, burning and yet unconsumed; or they who can say with St. Paul, "We are killed all the day long—dying, and behold we live!"

"Temptations," says Kempis,

> are often very profitable to men, though they be troublesome and grievous, for in them a man is humbled, purified, and instructed. All the saints have passed through and profited by many tribulations. And they that could not bear temptations, became reprobates and fell away.

"My son," adds the author of Ecclesiasticus (2:1)

> if thou come to serve the Lord [in the perfect beauty of holiness] prepare thy

soul for temptation. Set thy heart aright; constantly endure; and make not haste in the time of trouble. Whatever is brought upon thee, take cheerfully; and be patient when thou art changed to a low estate: for gold is tried and purified in the fire, and acceptable men in the furnace of adversity.

And therefore, says St. James, "Blessed is the man that endureth temptation; for, when he is tried, [if he stands the fiery trial] he shall receive the crown of life, which the Lord has promised to them that love him" [with the love which endureth all things, that is, with perfect love] (James 1:12). Patiently endure then, when God "for a season, if need be," allows you to be "in heaviness through manifold temptations." By this means, "the trial of your faith, being much more precious than that of gold which perisheth, though it be tried in the fire, will be found unto praise, and honor, and glory, at the appearing of Jesus Christ" (1 Peter 1:6-7).

Deep repentance is good, gospel self denial is excellent, and a degree of patient resignation in trials is of unspeakable use to attain the perfection of love. But as "faith *immediately* works by love," it is of far more immediate use to purify the soul. Hence it is that Christ, the prophets, and the apostles, so strongly insist upon faith, assuring us that "if we will not believe, we shall not be established," that "if we will believe, we shall see the glory of God; we shall be saved; and rivers of living water shall flow from our inmost souls; and that our hearts are purified by faith; and that we are saved by grace through faith." They tell us that

Christ gave himself for the Church, that he might sanctify and cleanse it…by the word; that he might present it to himself a glorious Church, not having spot, or wrinkle, or any such thing; but that it should be holy and without blemish.

Now, if believers are not to be "cleansed and made without blemish" by the word, (which testifies of the all-atoning blood, and the love of the Spirit) it is evident that they are to be sanctified by faith. Faith, or believing, has as necessary a reference to the word as eating has to food. For the same reason the apostle observes that "they who believe enter into rest; that a promise being given us to enter in, we should take care not to fall short of it" through unbelief; that we ought to take warning from the Israelites, who "could not enter" into the land of promise "through unbelief;" that we are "filled with all joy and peace in believing;" and that "Christ is able to save to the uttermost them who come unto God through him."

Now "coming," in Scriptural language, is another expression for *believing:* "He that cometh to God," says the apostle, "must believe." Hence it appears that faith is peculiarly necessary to those who will be saved to the uttermost, especially a firm faith in the singular promise of the Gospel of Christ, the promise of "the Spirit of holiness" from the Father, through the Son. For "how shall they call on him, in whom they have not believed?" Or how can they earnestly plead the truth and steadily wait for the performance of a promise in which they have no faith? This doctrine of faith is supported by Peter's words: "God, who knoweth the hearts [of penitent believers] bare them witness, giving them the Holy Ghost, and purifying their hearts by faith" (Acts 15:8-9). For the same Spirit of faith, which *initially* purifies our hearts when we cordially believe the pardoning love of God, *completely* cleanses them when we fully believe his sanctifying love.

This direction about faith being of the utmost importance, I shall confirm and explain it by an extract from Mr. Wesley's forty-third sermon, which points out the *Scripture Way of Salvation:* "Though it be allowed," says this judicious divine,

> that both this repentance and its fruits are necessary to full salvation, yet they are not necessary either in the same sense with faith, or in the same degree. *Not in the same degree,* for these fruits are only necessary conditionally, if there be time and opportunity for them. Otherwise a man may be sanctified without them. But he cannot be sanctified without faith. Likewise, let a man have ever so much of this repentance, or ever so many good works, yet all this does not at all avail. He is not sanctified till he believes. But the moment he believes, with or without those fruits, yes, with more or less of this repentance, he is sanctified. *Not in the same sense,* for this repentance and these fruits are only remotely necessary in order to the continuance of his faith, as well as the increase of it, whereas faith is immediately and directly necessary to sanctification. It remains that faith is the only condition which is immediately and directly necessary to sanctification.

> "But what is that faith whereby we are sanctified, saved from sin, and perfected in love?"

1. It is a Divine evidence and conviction, *that God hath promised it in the Holy Scriptures.* Till we are thoroughly satisfied of this, there is no moving one step farther. And one would imagine there needed not one word more to satisfy a reasonable man of this, than the ancient promise, "Then will I circumcise thy heart, and the heart of thy seed, to love the Lord thy God with all thy heart, and with all thy soul." How clearly this expresses the being perfected in love! How strongly it implies the being saved from all sin! For as long as love takes up the whole heart, what room is there for sin therein?

2. It is a Divine evidence and conviction, *that what God has promised he is able to perform.* Admitting, therefore, that "with men it is impossible to bring a clean thing out of an unclean," to purify the heart from all *sin,* and to fill it with all holiness; yet this creates no difficulty in the case, seeing "with God all things are possible."

3. It is an evidence and conviction *that he is able and willing to do it* NOW. And why not? Is not a moment to him the same as a thousand years? He cannot need more time to accomplish whatever is his will. We may therefore boldly say at any point of time, "Now is the day of salvation! Behold! All things are now ready! Come to the marriage!"

4. To this confidence, that God is both able and willing to sanctify us now, there needs to be added one thing more, a divine evidence and conviction *that he does it.* In that hour it is done. God says to the inmost soul, "According to thy faith, be it unto thee!" Then the soul is pure from every spot of sin. It is clean from all unrighteousness."

Those who have low ideas of faith will probably be surprised to see how much Mr. Wesley ascribes to that Christian grace, and to inquire why he so nearly connects our *believing that God cleanses us from all sin* with *God's actual cleansing us.* But their wonder will cease if they consider the definition which this divine gives of faith in the same sermon. "Faith, in general," says he,

is defined by the apostle as "evidence", a Divine evidence "and conviction [the word used by the apostle means both] of things not seen," not visible, nor perceivable either by sight, or by any other of the external senses. It implies both a supernatural evidence of God and of the things of God, a kind of *spiritual light* exhibited to the soul, and a *supernatural sight* or perception thereof. Accordingly the Scriptures speak of God's giving sometimes light, sometimes a power of discerning it. Thus St. Paul, "God who commanded light to shine out of darkness, hath shined in our hearts, to give us the light of the knowledge of the glory of God in the face of Jesus Christ." And elsewhere the same apostle speaks of "the eyes of our understanding being opened." By this twofold operation of the Holy Spirit, having the eyes of our souls both opened and enlightened, we see the things which the natural "eye hath not seen, neither the ear heard." We have a prospect of the invisible things of God. We see *the spiritual world* — which is all around us and yet is no more discerned by our natural faculties than if it had no being — and we see *the eternal world,* piercing through the veil which hangs between time and eternity. Clouds and darkness then rest upon it no more, but we already see the glory which shall be revealed.

From this striking definition of faith it is evident that the doctrine of this address exactly coincides with Mr. Wesley's sermon, with this verbal difference only: that what he calls faith, implying a two-fold operation of the Spirit, productive of *spiritual light and supernatural sight,* I have called faith, apprehending a sanctifying "baptism (or outpouring) of the Spirit." His mode of expression savors more of the rational divine who logically divides the truth in order to render its several parts conspicuous. I keep closer to the words of the Scriptures which, I hope, will frighten no candid Protestant. I make this remark for the sake of those who fancy that when a doctrine is clothed with expressions which are not quite familiar to them it is a new doctrine, although these expressions should be as Scriptural as those of a "baptism, or outpouring of the Spirit," which are used by some of the prophets, by John the Baptist, by the four evangelists, and by Christ himself.

I have already pointed out the close connection there is between an act of faith which fully apprehends the sanctifying promise of the Father and the power of the Spirit of Christ, which makes an end of moral corruption by forcing the lingering "man of sin" *instantaneously* to breathe out his last. Mr. Wesley, in the above-quoted sermon, touches upon this delicate subject in so clear and concise a manner, that while his discourse is before me, for the sake of those who have it not at hand, I shall transcribe the whole passage, and thus put the seal of that eminent divine to what I have advanced in the preceding pages, about sanctifying faith and the quick destruction of sin.

Does God work this great work in the soul *gradually* or *instantaneously?* Perhaps it may be gradually wrought in some; I mean, in this sense: they do not refer to the particular moment wherein sin ceases to be. But it is infinitely desirable, were it the will of God, that it should be done instantaneously; that the Lord should destroy sin "by the breath of his mouth," "in a moment, in the twinkling of an eye." And so he generally does, a plain fact of which there is evidence enough to satisfy any unprejudiced person.

You, therefore, look for it every moment. Look for it in the way above described, in all those good works to which you are created anew in Christ Jesus. There is then no danger. You can be no worse, if you are no better for that expectation. For were you to be disappointed of your hope, still you lose nothing.

But you shall not be disappointed of your hope. It will come, and will not tarry. Look for it then every day, every hour, every moment. Why not this hour, this moment? Certainly you may look for it now, if you believe it is by faith.

By this token you may surely know whether you seek it by faith or by works: if by *works,* you want something to be done first, before you are sanctified. You think, "I must first be or do thus or thus." Then you are seeking it by works unto this day.

If you seek it by *faith,* you expect it as you are, and if as you are, then expect it now. It is of importance to observe that there is an inseparable connection between these three points: expect it *by faith,* expect it as *you are,* and expect it *now!* To deny one of them is to deny them all. To allow one is to allow them all. Do you believe we are sanctified *by faith?* Be true then to your principle and look for this blessing just *as you are,* neither better nor worse, as a poor sinner that has still nothing to plead but *Christ died.* And if you look for it as you are, then expect it *now.* Stay for nothing. Why should you? Christ is ready, and he is all you need. He is waiting for you. He is at the door! Let your inmost soul cry out,

> *Come in, come in, thou heavenly Guest!*
> *Nor hence again remove:*
> *But sup with me, and let the feast*
> *Be everlasting love.*

Social prayer is closely connected with faith in the extraordinary promise of the sanctifying Spirit. Therefore I earnestly recommend that mean of grace, where it can be had, as being eminently conducive to the attaining of Christian perfection. When many believing hearts are lifted up and wrestle with God in prayer together, you may compare them to many diligent hands which work a large machine. At such times, particularly, the fountains of the great deep are broken up, the windows of heaven are opened, and "rivers of living water flow" into the hearts of obedient believers.

> *In Christ when brethren join,*
> *And follow after peace,*
> *The fellowship Divine*
> *He promises to bless,*
> *His chiefest graces to bestow*
> *Where two or three are met below.*
> *Where unity takes place,*
> *The joys of heaven we prove;*
> *This is the Gospel grace,*
> *The unction from above,*
> *The Spirit on all believers shed,*
> *Descending swift from Christ their Head.*

Accordingly we read, that when God powerfully opened the kingdom of the Holy Ghost on the day of Pentecost the disciples "were all with one accord in one place." And when he confirmed that kingdom, they "were lifting up their voices to God with one accord" (Acts 2:1; 4:24). Thus also the believers at Samaria were filled with the Holy Ghost, the Sanctifier, while Peter and John prayed with them and laid their hands upon them.

But perhaps you are alone. As a solitary bird which sits on the housetop, you look for a companion who may go with you through the deepest travail of the regeneration. But, alas! You look in vain. All the professors about you seem satisfied with their former experiences and with self-imputed or self-conceited perfection. When you give them a hint of your lack of power from on high and of your hunger and thirst after a fullness of righteousness, they do not sympathize with you. Indeed, how can they? They are full already. They reign without you. They have need of nothing. They do not sensibly want that

God would grant them, according to the riches of his glory, to be strengthened with might in the inner man, that Christ may dwell in their hearts by faith, that they, being rooted and grounded in love, may comprehend with all saints [perfected in love] what is the breadth, and length, and depth, and height, and to know the love of Christ which passeth knowledge, that they might be filled with all the fulness of God (Ephesians 3:16-19).

They look upon you as an erratic person, full of peculiar ideas, and they rather dampen than enliven your hopes. Your circumstances are sad, but do not give place to despair, no, not for a moment. In the name of Christ, who could not get even Peter, James and John, to watch with him one hour — and who was obliged to go through his agony alone — in his name, I say, "Cast not away thy confidence, which has great recompense of reward." Under all your discouragements remember that, after all, Divine grace is not confined to numbers any more than to a few. When all outward helps fail you, make the more of Christ, on whom sufficient help is laid for you — Christ, who says, "I will go with thee through fire and water; the former shall not burn thee, nor the latter drown thee." Jacob was alone when he wrestled with the angel, yet he prevailed; and "if the servant is not above his master" wonder not that it should be said of you as of your Lord, when he went through his greatest temptations, "of the people there was none with him."

Should your conflicts be "with confused noise, with burning and fuel of fire;" should your "Jerusalem be rebuilt in troublesome times;" should the Lord "shake not the earth only, but also heaven"; should "deep call unto deep at the noise of his waterspouts"; "should all his waves and billows go over thee;" should your patience be "tried to the uttermost;" remember how in years past you have tried the patience of God. Do not be discouraged. An extremity and a storm are often God's opportunity. A blast of temptation and a shaking of all your foundations may introduce the fullness of God to your soul and answer the end of the rushing wind, and of the shaking, which formerly accompanied the first great manifestations of the Spirit.

The Jews still expect the coming of the Messiah in the flesh, and they particularly expect it in a storm. When lightnings flash, when thunders roar, when a strong wind shakes their houses, and the tempestuous sky seems to rush down in thundershowers, then some of them particularly open their doors and windows to entertain their wished-for Deliverer. Do spiritually what they do carnally. Constantly wait for full "power from on high," but especially when a storm of affliction, temptation, or distress overtakes you. When your convictions and desires raise you above yourself, as the waters of the flood raised Noah's ark above the earth, then be particularly careful to throw open the door of *faith* and the window of *hope* as widely as you can. Spreading the arms of your imperfect *love*, say with all the ardor and resignation of which you art capable:

> *My heart strings groan with deep complaint,*
> *My flesh lies panting, Lord, for thee;*
> *And every limb, and every joint,*
> *Stretches for perfect purity.*

But if the Lord be pleased to come softly to your help; if he makes an end of your corruption by helping you gently to sink to unknown depths of meekness; if he drowns the indwelling man of sin by baptizing, by plunging him into an abyss of humility; do not find fault with the simplicity of his method, the plainness of his appearing, and the commonness of his prescription. Nature, like Naaman, is full of prejudices. She expects that Christ will come to make her clean with as much ado, pomp and bustle as the Syrian general looked for, "when he was wroth and said, 'Behold, I thought he will surely come out to me…and stand and call on his God…and strike his hand over the place…and recover the leper.'" Christ frequently goes a much plainer way to work and by this means he upsets all our preconceived notions and schemes of deliverance. "Learn of me to be meek and lowly in heart, and thou shalt find rest to thy soul," the sweet rest of Christian perfection, of perfect humility, resignation, and meekness. Lie at my feet, as she did who loved much, and was meekly taken up with "the good part, and the one thing needful." But you fret. You despise this robe of perfection. It is too plain for you. You slight "the ornament of a meek and quiet spirit which, in the sight of God, is of great price." Nothing will serve your turn but a gaudy coat of many colors, which may please your proud self-will and draw the attention of others by its glorious and flaming appearance. It must be brought to you with lightnings, thunderings, and voices.

If this be your disposition, wonder not at the Divine wisdom which thinks fit to disappoint your lofty prejudices. Let me address you as Naaman's servants addressed him: "My brother, if the prophet had told you to do some great thing, would you not have done it? How much rather then, when he says to you, *"I am the meek and lowly Lamb of God; wash in the stream of my blood—plunge in the Jordan of my humility, and be clean!"* Therefore, instead of going away from a plain Jesus in a rage, welcome him in his lowest appearance and be persuaded that he can as easily make an end of your sin by gently coming in "a still, small voice" as by rushing in upon you in "a storm, a fire, or an earthquake."

The Jews rejected their Savior, not so much because they did not earnestly desire his coming, as because he did not come in the manner in which they expected him. It is probable that some of this Judaism cleaves to you. If you will absolutely come to Mount Zion in a triumphal chariot, or make your entrance into the New Jerusalem upon a prancing horse, you are likely never to come there. Leave then all your lordly misconceptions behind and humbly follow your King, who makes his entry into the typical Jerusalem, "meek and lowly, riding upon an ass, yea, upon a colt, the foal of an ass."

I say it again, therefore, while your faith and hope strongly insist on the blessing, let your resignation and patience leave to God's infinite goodness and wisdom the peculiar manner of bestowing it. When he says, "Surely I come quickly to make my abode with thee," let your faith close in with his word, ardently and yet meekly embrace his promise. This will instantly beget power, and with that power you may instantly bring forth prayer, and possibly the prayer which opens heaven, humbly wrestles with God, inherits the blessing, and turns the well-known petition, "Amen! Even so, come Lord Jesus!" into the well-known praises, "He is come! He is come! O praise the Lord, O my *soul!"* etc. Thus repent, believe, and obey, and "he that cometh will come" with a fullness of pure, meek, humble love. "He will not tarry," or if he tarry, it will be to give your faith and desires more time to open, that you may at his appearing be able to take in more of his perfecting grace and sanctifying power. Besides, your expectation of his coming is of a purifying nature, and gradually sanctifies you. "He that has this hope in him," by this very hope "purifies himself even as God is pure," for "we are saved [into perfect love] by hope as well as by faith." The stalk, as well as the root, bears "the full corn in the ear."

Up then, sincere expectant of God's kingdom! Let yorur humble, ardent free will meet prevenient, sanctifying free grace in its weakest and darkest appearance, as the father of the faithful met the Lord, "when he appeared to him on the plain of Mamre" as a mere mortal. "Abraham lifted up his eyes and looked, and lo! three men stood by him." So does free grace (if I may venture upon the allusion) invite itself to your tent. Oh, no, it is now with you in its creating, redeeming, and sanctifying influences. "And when he saw them, he ran to meet them from the tent door, and bowed himself toward the ground." Go and do likewise. If you see any beauty in the humbling grace of our Lord Jesus Christ, in the sanctifying love of God, and in the comfortable fellowship of the Holy Ghost, let your free will run to meet them, and bow itself toward the ground.

O for a speedy going out of your tent, your sinful self! O for a race of desire in the way of faith! O for incessant prostrations! O for a meek and deep bowing of yourself before your Divine Deliverer! "And Abraham said, *My Lord, if now I have found favor in thy sight, pass not away, I pray thee, from thy servant!*" O for the humble pressing of a loving faith! O for the faith which stopped the sun, when God avenged his people in the days of Joshua! O for the importunate faith of the two disciples who detained Christ, when "he made as though he would have gone farther! They constrained him, saying, Abide with us, for it is toward evening, and *the day is far spent*. And he went in to tarry with them." He soon, indeed, vanished out of their bodily sight, because they were not called always to enjoy his bodily presence. Far from promising them that blessing, he had said,

It is expedient for you that I go away: for if I go not away, the Comforter will not come unto you; but if I depart, I will send him unto you, that he may abide with you for ever. He dwelleth with you, and shall be in you.

This promise is "*yea* and *amen* in Christ." Only plead it according to the preceding directions, and as sure as the Lord is the true and faithful Witness, so sure will the God of hope and love soon fill you with all joy and peace, that you may abound in pure love, as well as in confirmed hope, "through the power of the Holy Ghost."

Lift up your hands which hang down. Our Aaron, our heavenly High Priest, is near to hold them up. The spiritual Amalekites will not always prevail. Our Samuel, our heavenly prophet, is ready "to cut them and their king in pieces before the Lord. The promise is unto you." You are surely called to attain the perfection of your dispensation, although you still seem afar off. Christ, in whom that perfection centers — Christ, from whom it flows, is very near, even at the door. "Behold, says he [and this he spoke to Laodicean loiterers] I stand at the door and knock. If any man hear my voice and open, I will come in and sup with him," upon the fruits of my grace, in their Christian perfection, and he shall sup with me upon the fruits of my glory, in their angelical and heavenly maturity.

Hear this encouraging gospel:

> Ask, and you shall have; seek, and you shall find; knock, and it shall be opened unto you. For every one that asketh, receiveth; and he that seeketh, findeth; and to him that knocketh, it shall be opened. If any of you, [believers] lack wisdom—indwelling wisdom, [Christ the wisdom and the power of God dwelling in his heart by faith] let him ask of God, who giveth to all men, and upbraideth not, and it shall be given him. But let him ask [as a believer] in faith, nothing wavering; for he that wavereth is like a wave of the sea, driven with the wind and tossed: for let not that man think that he shall receive" the thing which he thus asketh. "But whatsoever things ye desire, when ye pray, believe that ye receive them, and ye shall have them. For all things [commanded and promised] are possible to him that believeth.

He who has commanded us to be perfect "in love, as our heavenly Father is perfect," and he who has promised "speedily to avenge his elect, who cry to him night and day;" will speedily avenge you of your great adversary, indwelling sin. He will say to you, "According to thy faith, be it done unto thee; for he is able to do far exceedingly abundantly, far above all that we can ask or think, and of his fullness we may all receive grace for grace" — we may all witness the gracious fulfillment of all the promises, which he has graciously made, that by "them we might be partakers of the Divine nature," so far as it can be communicated to mortals in this world.

You see that, with men, what you look for is impossible, but show yourselves believers. Take God into account, and you will soon experience that "with God all things are possible." Nor forget the omnipotent Advocate whom you have with him. Behold! He lifts his once pierced hands and says, "Father, sanctify them through thy [loving] truth, that they may be perfected in love:" and showing to you the fountain of atoning blood, and purifying water, from which flow the streams which cleanse and gladden the hearts of believers, he says, "*Hitherto you have asked* nothing in my name...whatsoever you shall ask the Father in my name, he will give it you. Ask, then, that your joy may be full." If I try your faith by a little delay, if I hide my face for a moment, it is only to gather you with everlasting kindness.

> A woman, when she is in travail, hath sorrow, because her hour is come: but as soon as she is delivered of the child, she remembereth no more the anguish for joy... now ye have sorrow, but I will see you again, and your hearts shall rejoice, and your joy no man taketh from you. In that day ye shall ask me no question, for you shall not have my bodily presence. But my urim and thummim will be with you; and the 'Spirit of truth' will himself lead you into all [Christian] truth.

> *O for a firm and lasting faith,*
> *To credit all the Almighty saith,*
> *To embrace the promise of his Son,*
> *And feel the Comforter our own!*

In the meantime, be not afraid to give glory to God by "believing in hope against hope." "Stagger not at the promise [of the Father and the Son] through unbelief," but trust the power and faithfulness of your Creator and Redeemer, till your Sanctifier has fixed his abode in your heart. Wait at mercy's door, as the lame beggar did at the beautiful gate of the temple. "Peter fastening his eyes upon him, with John, said, '*Look at us;*' and he gave heed to them, expecting to receive something of them." Do so, too. Give heed to the Father in the Son, who says, "Look unto me and be ye saved."

Expect to receive "the one thing now needful" for you, a fullness of the sanctifying Spirit, and though your patience may be tried, it shall not be disappointed. The faith and power which, at Peter's word, gave the poor cripple a perfect soundness in the presence of all the wondering Jews, will give you, at Christ's word, a perfect soundness of heart in the presence of all your adversaries.

> *Faith—mighty faith, the promise sees,*
> *And looks to that alone,*
> *Laughs at impossibilities,*
> *And cries, "It shall be done!'*

> *Faith asks impossibilities;*
> *Impossibilities are given:*
> *And I—e'en I, from sin shall cease,*
> *Shall live on earth the life of heaven.*

Faith always "works by love" — by love of desire at least — making us ardently pray for what we believe to be eminently desirable. If Christian perfection appears so to you, you might perhaps express your earnest desire of it in some such words as these: "How long, Lord, shall my soul, your spiritual temple, be a den of thieves, or a house of merchandise? How long shall vain thoughts profane it, as the buyers and sellers profaned your temple made with human hands? How long shall evil tempers lodge within me? How long shall unbelief, formality, hypocrisy, envy, hankering after sensual pleasure, indifference to spiritual delights, and backwardness to painful or ignominious duty, harbor there? How long shall these sheep and doves, yes, these goats and serpents, defile my breast, which should be pure as the holy of holies? How long shall they hinder me from being one of the worshippers whom you seek, one of those who worship you in spirit and in truth?

"O help me to take away these cages of unclean birds. 'Suddenly come to thy temple.' Turn out all that offends the eyes of your purity and destroy all that keeps me out of the rest which remains for your *Christian* people. So shall I keep a spiritual Sabbath, a Christian jubilee to the God of my life. So shall I witness my share in 'the oil of joy' with which you anoint perfect Christians above their fellow believers. I stand in need of that oil, Lord. My lamp burns dim. Sometimes it seems to be even gone out, like those of the foolish virgins. It is more like "a smoking flax" than "a burning and shining light." O! Quench it not! Raise it to a flame! You know that I do believe in you. The trembling hand of my faith holds you, and though I have ten thousand times grieved your pardoning love, your everlasting arm is still under me, to redeem my life from destruction, while your right hand is over me to crown me with mercies and lovingkindness.

"But, alas! I am neither sufficiently thankful for your present mercies, nor sufficiently athirst for your future favors. Hence I feel an aching void in my soul, being conscious that I have not attained the heights of grace described in your Word, and enjoyed by your holiest servants. Their deep experiences, the diligence and ardor with which they did your will, the patience and fortitude with which they endured the cross, reproach me and convince me of my many needs. I lack 'power from on high;' I lack the penetrating, lasting 'unction of the Holy One.'

"I need to have my vessel (my capacious heart) full of the oil, which makes the countenance of wise virgins cheerful. I want a lamp of heavenly illumination, and a fire of Divine love, burning day and night in my breast, as the lamps did in the temple, and the sacred fire on the altar. I desire a full application of the blood which cleanses from all sin, and a strong faith in your sanctifying Word, a faith by which you may dwell in my heart, as the unwavering hope of glory, and the fixed object of my love. I want the internal oracle, your still, small voice, together with *urim* and *thummim* [two Hebrew words which mean *lights and perfections*] —"the new name which none knoweth but he that receiveth it."

"In a word, Lord, I want a plenitude of your Spirit, the full promise of the Father, and the rivers which flow from the inmost souls of the believers who have gone on to the perfection of their dispensation. I do believe that you can and will thus "baptize me with the Holy Ghost and with fire." Help my unbelief. Confirm and increase my faith with regard to this important baptism. Lord, I have need to be thus baptized by you, and I am in difficulty till this baptism is accomplished. By your baptisms of tears in the manger, of water in the Jordan, of sweat in Gethsemane, of blood, and fire, and vapor of smoke, and flaming wrath on Calvary, baptize, O baptize my soul, and make as full an end of the original sin which I have from Adam as your last baptism made of the likeness of sinful flesh, which you had from a daughter of Eve.

Some of your people look at death for full salvation from sin but, at your command, Lord, I look to you. "Say to my soul, *I am thy salvation,"* and let me feel with my heart, as well as see with my understanding, that you can *save* from sin *to the uttermost, all that come to God through thee.* I am tired of forms, professions, and orthodox notions, inasmuch as they are not pipes or channels to convey life, light and love to my dead, dark and stony heart. Neither the plain letter of your gospel, nor the sweet foretastes and transient illuminations of your Spirit, can satisfy the large desires of my faith.

"Give me your abiding Spirit that he may continually shed abroad your love in my soul. Come, O Lord, with that blessed Spirit! Come, you and your Father, in that holy Comforter! Come make your abode with me, or I shall go meekly mourning to my grave. Blessed mourning! Lord, increase it. I had rather wait in tears for your fullness than immorally waste the fragments of your spiritual bounties, or feed with Laodicean contentment upon the tainted manna of my former experiences.

"Righteous Father, 'I hunger and thirst after thy righteousness!' Send your Holy Spirit of promise to fill me therewith, to sanctify me throughout, and to 'seal me *centrally* to the day of eternal redemption' and finished salvation. 'Not for works of righteousness which I have done, but of your mercy,' for Christ's sake, 'save me by the *complete* washing of regeneration, and the *full* renewing of the Holy Ghost.' And in order to do this, pour out of your Spirit. Shed it abundantly on me till the fountain of living water abundantly springs up in my soul and I can say, in the full sense of the words, that you live in me, that my life is 'hid with thee in God, and that my spirit is returned to him that gave it; to thee, the first and the last, my author and my end, my God and my all!'"

3

An Address to Perfect Christians

YOU HAVE NOT ASKED in vain, O men of God, who have mixed faith with your evangelical requests. The God who says, "Open thy mouth wide, and I will fill it;" the gracious God who declares, "Blessed are they that hunger after righteousness, for they shall be filled;" that faithful, covenant-keeping God has now filled you with all "righteousness, peace, and joy in believing." The brightness of Christ's appearing has destroyed the indwelling "man of sin." He who had slain the lion and the bear (he who had already done so great things for you) has now crowned all his blessings by slaying the Goliath within. Aspiring, unbelieving self is fallen before the victorious Son of David. The quick and powerful Word of God, which is sharper than any two-edged sword, has pierced even to the dividing asunder of soul and spirit. The carnal mind is cut off. The circumcision of the heart, through the Spirit, has fully taken place in your breasts, and now "that mind is in you which was also in Christ Jesus; ye are spiritually minded," loving God with all your heart, and your neighbor as yourselves. "Ye are full of goodness, ye keep the commandments," you observe *the law of liberty,* you fulfill *the law of Christ.* Of him you have "learned to be meek and lowly in heart." You have fully "taken his yoke upon you." In so doing you have found a sweet, abiding rest unto your souls, and from blessed experience ye can say, "Christ's yoke is easy, and his burden is light. His ways are ways of pleasantness, and all his paths are peace. All the paths of the Lord are mercy and truth, unto such as keep his covenant and his testimonies."

The beatitudes are sensibly yours, and the charity described by St. Paul has the same place in your breasts which the tables of the Law had in the Ark of the Covenant. You are the living temples of the

Trinity. The Father is your life, the Son your light, the Spirit your love. You are truly baptized into the mystery of God. You continue to "drink into one spirit," and thus you enjoy the grace of both sacraments. There is an end of your *Lo here!* and *Lo there!* The kingdom of God is now established within you. Christ's "righteousness, peace, and joy" are rooted in your breasts "by the Holy Ghost given unto you, as an abiding guide, and indwelling comforter. Your introverted eye of faith looks at God, who gently "guides you with his eye" into all the truth necessary to make you "do justice, love mercy, and walk humbly with your God."

Simplicity of intention keeps darkness out of your mind, and *purity of affection* keeps wrong fires out of your breast. By the former, you are without *guile;* by the latter, you are without *envy.* Your passive will instantly melts into the will of God, and on all occasions you meekly say, "Not my will, O Father, but yours be done!" Thus you are always ready to suffer what you are called to suffer. Your active will evermore says, "Speak, Lord; your servant hears: what would you have me to do? It is my meat and drink to do the will of my heavenly Father!" Thus are you always ready to do whatsoever you are convinced that God calls you to do, and whatsoever you do, whether you eat, or drink, or do anything else, you do all to the glory of God, and in the name of our Lord Jesus Christ; rejoicing evermore; praying without ceasing; in everything giving thanks; solemnly *looking for* and *hasting unto* the hour of your dissolution, and the "day of God, wherein the heavens, being on fire, shall be dissolved," and your soul, being clothed with a celestial body, shall be able to do celestial services to the God of your life.

In this blessed state of Christian perfection, the holy "anointing, which ye have received of him, abideth in you, and ye need not that any man teach you, unless it be as the same anointing teacheth." Agreeably, therefore, to that anointing, which teaches by a variety of means — which formerly taught a prophet by an ass and daily instructs God's children by the ant — I shall venture to set before you some important directions which the Holy Ghost has already suggested to your pure minds. "For I would not be negligent to put you in remembrance of these things, though ye know them, and be established in the present truth. Yea, I think it meet to stir you up, by putting you in remembrance," and giving you some hints, which it is safe for you frequently to meditate upon.

Adam, you know, lost his *human* perfection in paradise. Satan lost his *angelic* perfection in heaven. The devil thrust sore at Christ in the wilderness to throw him down from his *mediatorial* perfection. St. Paul, in the same epistles where he professes not only *Christian,* but *apostolic* perfection also (Philippians 3:15; 1 Corinthians 2:6; 2 Corinthians 12:11) informs us that he continued to "run for the crown of heavenly perfection" like a man who might not only lose his crown of Christian perfection, but become a reprobate, and be cast away, (1 Corinthians 9:25,27). Therefore, "so run ye also, that no man take your crown" of Christian perfection in this world, and that you may obtain your crown of angelic perfection in the world to come. Still keep your body under. Still guard your senses. Still watch your own heart and, "steadfast in the faith, still resist the devil that he may flee from you;" remembering that if Christ himself, as Son of man, had conferred with flesh and blood, refused to deny himself, and avoided taking up his cross, he had lost his perfection, and sealed up our original apostasy.

"We do not find," says Mr. Wesley, in his *Plain Account of Christian Perfection,*

> any general state described in Scripture, from which a man cannot draw back to sin. If there were any state wherein this is impossible, it would be that of those who are sanctified, who are fathers in Christ, who "rejoice evermore, pray without ceasing, and in everything give thanks." But it is not impossible for these to draw back. They who are sanctified may yet fall and perish (Hebrews 10:29). Even "fathers in Christ" need that warning, "Love not the world" (1 John 2:15). They who "rejoice, pray, and give thanks without ceasing" may nevertheless "quench the Spirit" (1 Thessalonians 5: 16) etc. No, even they who are "sealed unto the day of redemption," may yet "grieve the Holy Spirit of God" (Ephesians 4:30.)

The doctrine of the absolute perseverance of the saints is the first card which the devil played against man: "Ye shall not surely die, if ye break the law of your perfection." This fatal card won the game. Mankind and paradise were lost. The artful serpent had too well succeeded at his first game to forget that lucky card at his second. See him "transforming himself into an angel of light" on the pinnacle of the temple. There he plays over again his old game against the Son of God. Out of the Bible he pulls the very card which won our first parents, and swept the stakes—paradise—yes, swept it with the broom of destruction: "Cast thyself down," says he, "for it is written [that all things shall work together for your good, your very falls not excepted] he shall give his angels charge concerning thee, and in their *hands they shall bear thee up, lest at any time thou dash thy foot against a stone."* The tempter (thanks to Christ!) lost the game at that time, but he did not lose his card, and it is probable that he will play it against you all, only with some variation.

Let me mention one among a thousand: He promised our Lord that God's "angels should bear him up in their hands, if he threw himself down." It is not unlikely that he will promise you greater things still. Nor should I wonder if he was bold enough to hint that when you cast yourselves down, "God himself shall bear you up in his *hands*, yea, in his *arms* of everlasting love."

O men of God, learn wisdom by the fall of Adam. O anointed sons of the Most High, learn watchfulness by the conduct of Christ. If he was afraid to "tempt the Lord his God," will you dare to do it? If he rejected as poison the hook of the absolute perseverance of the saints, though it was baited with Scripture, will you swallow it down as if it were "honey out of the rock of ages?" No. Through faith in Christ the Scriptures have made you "wise unto salvation." You will not only flee with all speed from evil, but from the very appearance of evil, and when you stand on the brink of a temptation, far from "entering into it" under any pretence whatever, you will leap back into the bosom of him who says, "Watch and pray, lest ye enter into temptation; for though the spirit is willing, the flesh is weak." I grant that, evangelically speaking, "the weakness of the flesh" is not sin, but yet the "deceitfulness of sin" creeps in at this door and in this way not a few of God's children, "after they had escaped the pollutions of the world, through the [sanctifying] knowledge of Christ", under plausible pretences, have been "entangled again therein and overcome." Let their falls make you cautious. You have "put on the whole armor of God." O keep it on, and use it "with all prayer," that you may to the last "stand complete in Christ, and be more than conquerors through him that has loved you."

Remember that "everyone who is perfect shall be as his Master." Now if your Master was tempted and assaulted *to the last;* if *to the last* he watched and prayed, using all the means of grace himself, and enforcing the use of them upon others; if *to the last* he fought against the world, the flesh, and the devil, and did not "put off the harness" till he had put off the body; think not yourselves above him; but "go and do likewise." If he did not regain Paradise without going through the most complete renunciation of all the good things of this world, and without meekly submitting to the severe stroke of his last enemy, death, be content to be "perfect as he was." Do not fancy that your flesh and blood can inherit the celestial kingdom of God when the flesh and blood which Emmanuel himself assumed from a pure virgin could not inherit it without passing under the cherub's flaming sword—I mean, without going through the gates of death.

You are not complete in wisdom. Perfect love does not imply perfect knowledge but perfect humility, and perfect readiness to receive instruction. Remember, therefore, that if ever you show that you are above being instructed, even by a fisherman who teaches according to the Divine anointing, you will show that you are fallen from a perfection of humility into a perfection of pride.

Do not confound angelical with Christian perfection. Uninterrupted transports of praise and ceaseless raptures of joy do not belong to Christian but to angelical perfection. Our feeble frame can bear but a few drops of that glorious cup. In general, that *new wine* is too strong for our *old bottles.* That power is too excellent for our earthen, cracked vessels. But weak as they are, they can bear a fullness of meekness, of resignation, of humility, and of that love which is willing to "obey unto death." If God indulge you with ecstacies and extraordinary revelations be thankful for them, but be "not exalted above measure by them." Take care lest enthusiastic delusions mix themselves with them. Remember that your Christian perfection does not so much consist in "building a tabernacle" upon Mount Tabor, to rest and enjoy rare sights there, as in resolutely taking up the cross and following Christ to the palace of a proud Caiaphas, to the judgment hall of an unjust Pilate, and to the top of an ignominious Calvary.

You never read in your Bibles, "Let that glory be upon you which was also upon St. Stephen, when he looked up steadfastly into heaven, and said, *'Behold! I see the heavens opened, and the Son of man standing on the right hand* of God.'" But you have frequently read there, "Let this mind be in you, which was also in Christ Jesus, who made himself of no reputation, took upon him the form of a servant, and being found in fashion as a man, humbled himself, and became obedient unto death, even the death of the cross."

See him on that ignominious gibbet! He hangs, abandoned by his friends, surrounded by his foes, condemned by the rich, insulted by the poor! He hangs, a worm and no man, a very scorn of men, and the outcast of the people! All that see him laugh him to scorn! They shoot out their lips and shake their heads, saying, "He trusted in God, that he would deliver him; let him deliver him, if he will have him!" There is none to help him. One of his apostles denies, another sells him, and the rest run away.

Many oxen are come about him. Fat bulls of Bashan close him on every side. They gape upon him with their mouths like a ramping lion. He is poured out like water. His heart in the midst of his body is like melting wax. His strength is dried up like a potsherd. His tongue cleaves to his gums. He is going into the dust of death. Many dogs are come about him, and the counsel of the wicked lays siege against him. His hands and feet are pierced. You may count all his bones. They stand staring and looking upon him. They divide his garments among them, and cast lots for the only remains of his property — his plain, seamless vesture.

Both suns, the visible and the invisible, seem eclipsed. No cheering beam of created light brightens his gloomy prospect. No smile of his heavenly Father supports his agonizing soul! No cooling drink, unless it be vinegar and gall, revives his sinking spirits! He has nothing left except his God. But his God is enough for him. In his God he has all things. And though his soul is seized with sorrow, even to death, yet it hangs more firmly upon his God by a naked faith than his lacerated body does on the cross by the clenched nails. The perfection of his love shines in all its Christian glory. He not only forgives his insulting foes and bloody persecutors but, in the highest point of his passion, he forgets his own wants and thirsts after their eternal happiness. Together with his blood he pours out his soul for them and, excusing them all, he says, "Father, forgive them, for they know not what they do." O you adult sons of God, in this mirror behold all with open face the glory of your Redeemer's forgiving, praying love and, as you behold it, be changed into the same image from glory to glory, by the loving Spirit of the Lord.

This lesson is deep, but he may teach you one deeper still. By a strong sympathy with him in all his sufferings he may call you to "know him *every way* crucified." Stern justice thunders from heaven, "Awake, O sword, against the man who is my fellow!" The sword awakes. The sword goes through his soul. The flaming sword is quenched in his blood. But is one sinew of his perfect faith cut, one fiber of his perfect resignation injured by the astonishing blow? No, his God slays him and yet he trusts in his God. By the noblest of all ventures, in the most dreadful of all storms, he meekly bows his head, and shelters his departing soul in the bosom of his God. *"My God, my God!"* says he, "though all my comforts have forsaken me, and all your storms and waves go over me, yet 'into thy hands I commend my spirit. For thou wilt not leave my soul in hell; neither wilt thou suffer thy Holy One to see corruption. Thou wilt show me the path of life, in thy presence is fulness of joy, and at thy right hand [where I shall soon sit] there are pleasures for evermore.'"

What a pattern of perfect confidence! O you perfect Christians, be ambitious to ascend to those amazing heights of Christ's perfection,

> for hereunto are ye called; because Christ also suffered for us; leaving us an example, that we should follow his steps, who knew no sin; who, when he was reviled, reviled not again; when he suffered he threatened not, but committed himself to him that judgeth righteously.

If this be your high calling on earth, rest not, O fathers in Christ, till your patient hope and perfect confidence in God have got their last victory over your last enemy, the king of terrors. "The ground of a thousand mistakes," says Mr. Wesley,

> is the not considering deeply that love is the highest gift of God, *humble, gentle, patient love;* that all visions, revelations, manifestations whatever, are little things compared to love. It were well you should be thoroughly sensible of this. The heaven of heavens is love. There is nothing higher in religion. There is, in effect, nothing else. If you look for anything but more love, you are looking wide of the mark. You are getting out of the royal way. And when you are asking others, "Have you received this or that blessing?" if you mean anything but *more love,* you mean wrong. You are leading them out of the way, and putting them upon a false scent. Settle it then in your heart, that from the moment God has saved you from all sin, you are to aim at nothing *but more of that* love described in the thirteenth chapter of First Corinthians. You can go no higher than this, till you are carried into Abraham's bosom.

Love is humble. "Be, therefore, clothed with humility," says Mr. Wesley:

> Let it not only fill, but cover you all over. Let modesty and self-aversion appear in all your words and actions. Let all you speak and do show that you are little, and base, and inferior, and vile in your own eyes. As one instance of this, be always ready to acknowledge any fault you have. If you have at any time, thought, spoken, or acted wrongly, be not backward to acknowledge it. Never dream that this will hurt the cause of God. No, it will further it. Therefore, be open and frank when you are charged with anything. Let it appear just as it is and you will thereby not hinder, but adorn the Gospel.

Why should you be more backward in acknowledging your failings than in confessing that you do not pretend to infallibility? St. Paul was perfect in the love which casts out fear, and therefore he boldly reproved the high priest. But when he had reproved him more sharply than the fifth commandment allows, he directly confessed his mistake, and set his seal to the importance of the duty, in which he had been inadvertently lacking. Then Paul said, "I knew not, brethren, that he was the high priest: for it is written, Thou shalt not speak evil of the ruler of thy people."

St. John was perfect in the courteous, humble love which brings us down at the feet of all. His courtesy, his humility, and the dazzling glory which beamed forth from a divine messenger (whom he apprehended to be more than a creature) betrayed him into a fault contrary to that of St. Paul. But far from concealing it, he openly confessed it and published his confession for the edification of all the Churches. "When I had heard and seen," says he, "I fell down to worship before the feet of the angel who showed me these things. Then saith he unto me, 'See thou do it not, for I am thy fellow servant'." Christian perfection shines as much in the childlike simplicity with which the perfect readily acknowledge their faults, as it does in the manly steadiness with which they "resist unto blood, striving against sin."

If humble love makes us frankly confess our faults, much more does it incline us to own ourselves sinners, miserable sinners before that God whom we have so frequently offended. I need not remind you that your "bodies are dead because of sin." You see, you feel it, and therefore, so long as you dwell in a prison of flesh and blood, which death, the avenger of sin, is to pull down; so long as your final justification, as pardoned and sanctified sinners, has not taken place: yes, so long as you break the law of paradisiacal perfection, under which you were originally placed, it is appropriate, right, and your bound duty to consider yourselves as sinners who, as transgressors of the law of innocence and the law of liberty, are guilty of death, of eternal death.

St. Paul did so after he was "come to Mount Zion, and to the spirits of just men made perfect." He still looked upon himself as the chief of sinners, because he had been a daring blasphemer of Christ, and a fierce persecutor of his people. "Christ," says he, "came to save sinners, of whom I am chief." The reason is plain. Matter of fact is, and will be matter of fact to all eternity. According to the doctrines of grace and justice, and before the throne of God's mercy and holiness, a sinner pardoned and sanctified must, in the very nature of things, be considered as a sinner; for if you consider him as a saint, absolutely abstracted from the character of a sinner, how can he be a pardoned and sanctified sinner?

To all eternity, therefore, but much more while death (the wages of sin) is at your heels, and while you are going to "appear before the judgment seat of Christ", to receive your final sentence of absolution or condemnation, it will become you to say with St. Paul, "We have all sinned, and come short of the glory of God; being justified freely [as sinners] by his grace, through the redemption that is in Jesus Christ." We are justified *judicially as believers,* through faith — *as obedient believers,* through the obedience of faith — and as *perfect Christians,* through Christian perfection.

Humble love "becomes all things [but sin] to all men," although it delights most in those who are most holy. You may, and ought to, set your love of peculiar complacence upon God's dearest children, upon "those who excel in virtue," because they more strongly reflect the image of "the God of love, the Holy One of Israel." But if you despise the weak and are above lending them a helping hand, you are fallen from Christian perfection, which teaches us to "bear one another's burdens," especially the burdens of the weak. Imitate, then, the tenderness and wisdom of the good Shepherd who "carries the lambs in his bosom, gently leads the sheep which are big with young," feeds with milk those who cannot bear strong meat, and says to his imperfect disciples, "I have many things to say to you, but ye cannot bear them now."

"Where the *loving* Spirit of the Lord is, there is liberty." Keep therefore at the utmost distance from the shackles of a narrow, prejudiced, bigoted spirit. The moment you confine your love to the people who think just as you do, and your regard to the preachers who exactly suit your taste, you fall from perfection and turn bigots. "I entreat you," says Mr. Wesley, in his *Plain Account,*

> beware of bigotry. Let not your love or beneficence be confined to *Methodists* (so called) only — much less to that very small part of them who seem to be renewed in love — or to those who believe yours and their report. O make not this your Shibboleth.

On the contrary, as you have time and ability, "do good to all men." Let your benevolence shine upon all. Let your charity send its cherishing beams toward all, in proper degrees. So shall you be perfect as your heavenly Father, "who makes his sun to shine upon all," although he sends the brightest and warmest beams of his favor upon "the household of faith," and reserves his richest bounties for those who lay out their five talents to the best advantage.

Love, pure love, is satisfied with the Supreme Good—with *God*.

Beware then of desiring anything but him. Now you desire nothing else. Every other desire is driven out. See that none enter in again. "Keep yourself pure: let your eye *remain* single, and your whole body shall remain full of light." Admit no desire of pleasing food, or any other pleasure of sense; no desire of pleasing the eye or imagination; no desire of money, of praise, or esteem; of happiness in any creature. You may bring these desires back, but you need not. You may feel them no more. "O stand fast in the liberty wherewith Christ hath made you free!" Be patterns to all of denying yourselves and taking up your cross daily. Let them see that you make no account of any pleasure which does not bring you nearer to God, nor regard any pain which does; that you simply aim at pleasing him, whether by doing or suffering; that the constant language of your heart with regard to pleasure or pain, honor or dishonor, is—

> *All's alike to me, so I*
> *In my Lord may live and die!*

The best soldiers are sent upon the most difficult and dangerous expeditions. As you are the best soldiers of Jesus Christ, you will probably be called to drink deepest of his cup, and to carry the heaviest burdens. "Expect contradiction and opposition," says the judicious divine, whom I have just quoted,

together with crosses of various kinds. Consider the words of St. Paul: "To you it is given in behalf of Christ," for his sake, as a fruit of his death and intercession for you, "not only to believe, but also to suffer for his sake," (Philippians 1:29).

It is given! God *gives* you this opposition or reproach. It is a fresh token of his love. Will you disown the giver? Or spurn his gift, and count it a misfortune? Will you not rather say, "Father, the hour is come, that thou shouldst be glorified. Now thou givest thy child to suffer something for thee. Do with me according to thy will." Know that these things, far from being *hindrances* to the work of God, or to your souls, unless by your own fault, are not only unavoidable in the course of Providence, but *profitable* — yes, *necessary* — for you. Therefore receive them from God (not from chance) with willingness and thankfulness. Receive them from men with humility, meekness, yieldingness, gentleness, sweetness.

Love can never do nor suffer too much for its Divine object. Be then ambitious, like St. Paul, to be made perfect in *sufferings*. I have already observed that the apostle, not satisfied to be a perfect Christian, would also be a perfect martyr, earnestly desiring to "know the fellowship of Christ's sufferings." Follow him, as he followed his suffering, crucified Lord. Your feet "are shod with the preparation of the Gospel of peace." Run after them both in the race of obedience, for the crown of martyrdom if that crown is reserved for you. And if you miss the crown of those who are martyrs in *deed,* you shall, however, receive the reward of those who are martyrs in *intention*— the crown of righteousness and angelical perfection.

But do not so desire to follow Christ to the garden of Gethsemane as to refuse following him *now* to the carpenter's shop, if Providence *now* calls you to it. Do not lose *the present day* by idly looking back at *yesterday,* or foolishly anticipating the cares of *tomorrow.* Wisely use every hour; spending it as one who stands on the verge of time, on the border of eternity, and one who has his work cut out by a wise Providence from moment to moment. Never, therefore, neglect using the two talents you have *now,* and doing the duty which is *now* incumbent upon you. Should you be tempted to it, under the plausible pretence of waiting for a greater number of talents, remember that God doubles our talents in the way of duty, and that it is a maxim, advanced by Elisha Coles himself, "Use grace and have [more] grace."

Therefore, "to continual watchfulness and prayer, add continual employment," says Mr. Wesley,

> for grace fills a vacuum as well as nature. The devil fills whatever God does not fill...*As by works faith is made perfect,* so the completing or destroying of the work of faith, and enjoying the favor or suffering the displeasure of God, greatly depend on every single act of obedience.

If you forget this, you will hardly do *now* whatever your hand finds to do. Much less will you do it with *all* your might, for God, for eternity.

Love is modest. It rather inclines to bashfulness and silence than to talkative forwardness. "In a multitude of words there wanteth not sin." Be therefore "slow to speak," nor cast your pearls before those who cannot distinguish them from pebbles. Nevertheless, when you are solemnly called upon to bear testimony to the truth, and to say "what great things God has done for you," it would be cowardice, or false prudence, not to do it with humility. Be then "always ready to give an answer to every man who [properly] asketh you a reason of the hope that is in you, with meekness [without fluttering anxiety] and with fear [with a reverential awe of God upon your minds]" (1 Peter 3:15).

Perfect Christians are "burning and shining lights." Our Lord intimates that as "a candle is not lighted to be put under a bushel, but upon a candlestick, that it may give light to all the house," so God does not light the candle of perfect love to hide it in a corner, but to give light to all those who are within the reach of its brightness. If diamonds glitter, if stars shine, if flowers display their colors, and perfumes diffuse their fragrance, to the honor of the Father of lights, and Author of every good gift; if, without self-seeking, they disclose his glory to the utmost of their power, why should "ye *not* go and do likewise?" Gold answers its most valuable end when it is brought to light, and made to circulate for charitable and pious uses, and not when it lies concealed in a miser's strongbox or in the dark bosom of a mine. But when you lay out your spiritual gold for proper uses, beware of imitating the vanity of those showoffs who, as often as they are about to pay for a trifle, pull out a handful of gold, merely to make a show of their wealth.

Love or "charity rejoiceth in the [display of an edifying] truth." Fact is fact, all the world over. If you can say to the glory of God, that *you are alive and feel very well,* when it is so, why should you not also testify to his honor that you "live not, but that Christ liveth in you," if you really find that this is your experience? Did not St. John say, "Our love is made perfect, because as he is, so are we in this world?" Did not St. Paul write, "The righteousness of the law is fulfilled in us, who walk after the Spirit?" Did he not, with the same simplicity, declare, that although "he had nothing, and was sorrowful, yet he possessed all things, and was always rejoicing?"

Hence it appears that, with respect to the declaring or concealing what God has done for your soul, the line of your duty runs exactly between *the proud forwardness* of some stiff Pharisees, and *the voluntary humility* of some stiff mystics. The former vainly boast of more than they experience, and thus set up the cursed idol, *Self*: The latter ungratefully hide "the wonderful works of God," which the primitive Christians spoke of publicly in a variety of languages, and so refuse to exalt their gracious benefactor, *Christ.* The first error is undoubtedly more odious than the second, but what need is there of leaning to either? Would you avoid them both?

Let your tempers and lives always declare that perfect love is attainable in this life. And when you have a proper call to declare it with your lips and pens, do it without forwardness, to the glory of God. Do it with simplicity, for the edification of your neighbor. Do it with godly jealousy, lest you should show the treasures of divine grace in your hearts with the same *self-complacence* with which King Hezekiah showed his treasures and the golden vessels of the temple to the ambassadors of the king of Babylon. Remember what a dreadful curse this piece of vanity pulled down upon him:

> And Isaiah said unto Hezekiah, Hear the word of the Lord, Behold the days come, that all that is in thine house shall be carried into Babylon: nothing shall be left, saith the Lord.

If God so severely punished Hezekiah's pride, how properly does St. Peter charge believers to "give with fear an account of the grace which is in them!" and how careful should you be to observe this important charge!

If you will keep at the utmost distance from the vanity which proved so fatal to good King Hezekiah, follow an excellent direction of Mr. Wesley. When you have done anything for God, or received any favor from him, retire, if not into your *closet,* into your *heart,* and say, "I come, Lord, to restore to you what you have given, and I freely relinquish it, to enter again into my own nothingness. For what is the most perfect creature in heaven or earth in your presence but a void, capable of being filled with you and by you, as the air which is void and dark is capable of being filled with the light of the sun? Grant therefore, O Lord, that I may never appropriate your grace to myself, any more than the air appropriates to itself the light of the sun which withdraws it every day to restore it the next, there being nothing in the air that either appropriates his light or resists it. O give me the same facility of receiving and restoring your grace and good works!

I say "yours," for I acknowledge that the root from which they spring is in *you*, and not in *me*."

> The true means to be filled anew with the riches of grace is thus to strip ourselves of it; without this it is extremely difficult not to faint in the practice of good works... And therefore, that your good works may receive their last perfection, let them lose themselves in God. This is a kind of death to them, resembling that of our bodies, which will not attain their highest life, their immortality, till they lose themselves in the glory of our souls, or rather of God, with which they shall be filled. And it is only what they had of earthly and mortal, which good works lose by this spiritual death.

Would you see this deep precept put in practice? Consider St. Paul. Already possessed of Christian perfection, he does good works from morning till night. He warns everyone night and day with tears. He carries the gospel from east to west. Wherever he stops, he plants a church at the hazard of his life. But instead of resting in his present perfection and in the good works which spring from it, "he grows in grace, and in the knowledge of our Lord Jesus Christ;" unweariedly "following after, if that he may apprehend that [perfection] for which also he is apprehended of Christ Jesus" — that celestial perfection of which he got lively ideas when he was "caught up to the third heaven, and heard unspeakable words, which it is not possible for a man to utter." With what amazing passion does he run his race of Christian perfection for the prize of that higher perfection! How he forgets the works of yesterday, in laying himself out for God today! "Though dead, he yet speaketh," nor can an address to perfect Christians be closed by a more proper speech than his. "Brethren," says he,

> be followers of me...I count not myself to have apprehended [my ultimate perfection] but this one thing I do, forgetting those things which are behind [settling in none of my former experiences, resting in none of my good works] and reaching forth unto those things which are before, I press toward the mark for the [celestial] prize of the high calling of God in Christ Jesus. Let us therefore, as many as are perfect, be thus minded; and if in any- thing ye be otherwise minded, God shall reveal even this unto you.

In the meantime you may sing the following hymn of the Rev. Mr. Charles Wesley, which is descriptive of the destruction of corrupt self-will, and expressive of the absolute resignation which characterizes a perfect believer:

To do, or not to do; to have,
  Or not to have, I leave to thee:
To be or not to be, I leave:
  Thy only will be done in me!
All my requests are lost in one,
  "Father, thy only will be done!"

Suffice that for the season past,
  Myself in things Divine I sought;
For comforts cried with eager haste,
  And murmur'd that I found them not
I leave it now to thee alone,
  Father, thy only will be done!

Thy gifts I clamor for no more,
  Or selfishly thy grace require,
An evil heart to varnish o'er:
  Jesus, the giver, I desire,
After the flesh no longer known:
  Father, thy only will be done!

Welcome alike the crown or cross,
  Trouble I cannot ask, nor peace,
Nor toil, nor rest, nor gain, nor loss,
  Nor joy, nor grief, nor pain, nor ease,
Nor life, nor death; but ever groan,
  "Father, thy only will be done!"

This hymn suits all the believers who are at the bottom of Mount Zion, and begin to join "the spirits of just men made perfect." But when the triumphal chariot of perfect love *gloriously* carries you to the top of perfection's hill; when you are raised far above the *common* heights of the perfect; when you are almost translated into glory, like Elijah, then you may sing another hymn of the same Christian poet:

Who in Jesus confide,
  They are bold to outride
All the storms of affliction beneath:
  With the prophet they soar
To that heavenly shore,
  And outfly all the arrows of death.

By faith we are come
  To our permanent home;
And by hope we the rapture improve:
  By love we still rise,
And look down on the skies—
  For the heaven of heavens is love!

Who on earth can conceive,
  How happy we live
In the city of God, the great King?
  What a concert of praise,
When our Jesus's grace
  The whole heavenly company sing!

What a rapturous song,
  When the glorified throng
In the spirit of harmony join!
  Join all the glad choirs,
Hearts, voices, and lyres,
  And the burden is mercy Divine!

But when you cannot rise to those rapturous heights of perfection, you need not give up your shield. You may still rank among the perfect, if you can heartily join in this version of Psalm 131:

Lord, thou dost the grace impart!
  Poor in spirit, meek in heart,
I shall as my Master be,
  Rooted in humility.

Now, dear Lord, that thee I know,
  Nothing will I seek below,
Aim at nothing great or high,
  Lowly both in heart and eye.

Simple, teachable, and mild,
  Awed into a little child,
Quiet now without my food,
  Wean'd from every creature good.

Hangs my new-born soul on thee,
  Kept from all idolatry;
Nothing lacks beneath, above,
  Resting in thy perfect love.

That your earthen vessels may be filled with this love till they break, and you enjoy the divine object of your faith without an interposing veil of gross flesh and blood, is the wish of one who sincerely praises God on your account, and fervently prays:

Make up thy Jewels, Lord, and show
  The glorious, spotless Church below:
The fellowship of saints make known;
  And O! my God, might I be one!

O might my lot be cast with these,
  The least of Jesus' witnesses!
O that my Lord would count me meet,
  To wash his dear disciples' feet!

To wait upon his saints below!
  On Gospel errands for them go!
Enjoy the grace to angels given;
  And serve the royal heirs of heaven!

4

A Letter by Thomas Rutherford

To a Friend in London
York, 1787

MY DEAR FRIEND: You ask, "Do I think there are degrees in sanctification?" I certainly do. And "what is the lowest degree thereof?" Sanctification begins at justification. In the same moment that we are justified, we are also born again, and therefore sanctified in part. But you mean *entire* sanctification. The lowest degree of this, in the very nature of the thing, is the being cleansed from all inbred sin; from unbelief, pride, anger, peevishness, murmuring, sinful self-love, foolish desires, and undue attachments to persons and things; from all that is contrary to the love of God and our neighbor to the mind which was also in Christ Jesus.

Whatever remains in us contrary to these is properly sin and, of consequence, so far we are not sanctified. We may be *entirely* sanctified and yet tempted to sin, for sin and temptation are essentially different. Our Lord was tempted to despair, presumption and apostasy. That is, the temptation was offered, the bait was laid for Him, but He totally rejected it. He has nowhere promised to exempt us from temptation, but only that with the temptation He will made a way of our escape that we may be able to bear it. If when we are tempted — let the temptation be what it may — we steadfastly follow our Lord's example and, like Him, resist and reject it, we do not sin, but conquer through Him that loved us. On the other hand, if sin in any degree remains in our heart, we are not *entirely* sanctified; sanctification in this sense being nothing less than the destruction of all indwelling sin.

Perhaps you will say, "If this be the lowest degree of *entire* sanctification, what is the highest degree of it?" I answer, Having the same mind which was also in Christ Jesus; being filled with all the fullness of God; living and dying complete in the will of Him who has called us to His kingdom and glory. The highest degree of sanctification is prayed for, by our Lord in behalf of all that believe on Him (John 17:20-26). The fruits of it are described by Him in His sermon on the mount, particularly in Matthew 5:44-48; by St. Paul, 1 Corinthians 13:4-7; by St. James, 3:17; by St. Peter, 2 Epistle 1:5-9; and by St. John, 1 Epistle 2:3-10; 3:21-24; 4:16-21. I shall only here insert the words of St. John, which are,

Hereby we do know that we know him, if we keep his commandments. He that saith, I know him, and keepeth not his commandments, is a liar, and the truth is not in him. But whoso keepeth his word, in him verily is the love of God perfected: hereby know we that we are in him. He that saith he abideth in him ought himself also so to walk, even as he walked. He that loveth his brother abideth in the light and there is none occasion of stumbling in him. Beloved, if our heart condemn us not, then have we confidence toward God. And whatsoever we ask, we receive of him, because we keep his commandments, and do those things that are pleasing in his sight: and this is his commandment, that we should believe on the name of his Son Jesus Christ, and love one another, as he gave us commandment. And he that keepeth his commandments dwelleth in him, and he in him. And hereby we know that he abideth in us, by the Spirit which he hath given us. We have known and believed the love that God hath to us. God is love; and he that dwelleth in love, dwelleth in God, and God in him. Herein is our love made perfect, that we may have boldness in the day of judgment: because as he is, so are we in this world. There is no fear in love; but perfect love casteth out fear: because fear hath torment. He that feareth is not made perfect in love. We love him because he first loved us. If a man say, I love God, and hateth his brother, he is a liar: for he that loveth not his brother whom he hath seen, how can he love God whom he hath not seen? And this commandment have we from him, That he who loveth God, loveth his brother also.

He who bears these fruits is a father in Christ.

St. Paul had attained the very summit of Christian perfection, not only as it respects *receiving*, but also *doing* and *suffering* the will of God, when he testified,

I am now ready to be offered, and the time of my departure is at hand. I have fought a good fight, I have finished my course, I have kept the faith. Henceforth there is laid up for me a crown of righteousness, which the Lord, the righteous Judge, shall give me at that day (Timothy 4:6-8).

If any ask how he attained to all this, he tells them. Philippians 3:13, 14: "This one thing I do, forgetting those things which are behind, and reaching forth unto those which are before, I press toward the mark for the prize of the high calling of God in Christ Jesus.

Perhaps some may think I place the mark too high, but I hope it is no higher than the Scriptures place it and I dare not fix it any lower.

"But may it not discourage some from seeking after it?" It *may*, but it *need* not, there being no *just* cause why it should. The Lord is as able to bring all His faithful children to the greatest depths and height of holiness as He was to bring the children of Israel into the Promised Land. He can as easily remove and cast down whatever opposes them as he divided Jordan and overthrew the walls of Jericho. Whoever, like Caleb and Joshua, follow him fully, shall be brought into the wealthy place. They shall be redeemed from all iniquity and filled with all the fullness of God. All discouragement vanishes when we consider—

First: This great salvation is all from the Lord, with whom all things are possible. He speaks and it is done. He commands and it stands fast. He says, "I will. Be thou clean," and immediately the leprosy of sin departs. "Behold, I make all things new!" and lo! a new creation of light, life, love, holiness, and happiness arises in the heart, "where only Christ is heard to speak, where Jesus reigns alone."

Secondly: It is all received by faith. The penitent and obedient believer sees the word, the promise, the oath of Him who cannot lie; firmly (as well he may) believes the truth thereof; steadfastly and in the full confidence of hope looks to the *promise-making* and *promise-fulfilling* God, being fully persuaded that what He has promised He is both able and willing *now* to perform; and according to his faith it is done unto him. By believing with his whole heart unto righteousness, he sets to his seal that God is true, and God seals him with the Holy Ghost sent down from heaven, thereby stamping his whole image upon his soul. Thus,

Faith, mighty faith, the promise sees,
And looks to that alone;
Laughs at impossibilities,
And cries, It shall be done.

Meantime we have infinite need to let whatever grace we have received be seen in us more by its own fruits than by our talk concerning it. The blessed Jesus is our pattern. Let us study His holy life day and night and seek, in all things, a perfect conformity to Him who, though He was equal with God, was content to be as "a worm and no man, made himself of no reputation; took upon him the form of a servant; and became obedient unto death, even the death of the cross."

He is the most perfect Christian who is most like his humble, patient, loving, and obedient Lord and Savior. I think some persons among us have been hurt by being set up and extolled for their great attainments in religion. Christ is the "Lily of the valleys." He dwells in humble hearts. It is good to lie low, and leave it to the Lord either to exalt or depress us as He shall see best. I do not write this because I think my friend in particular danger from that quarter; by no means. But humility is a lesson which we all need to be daily learning, and I write to her just as I think for myself.

I am sure you agree with me in believing that the late Mr. Fletcher was the holiest person you ever saw; the person who, above all others, excelled most in every grace. Yet he made no account of himself in anything. He was indeed "clothed with humility."

That we may be followers of him as he was of Christ is the prayer of —

Your sincere friend,
T. R.

About the Author...

JOHN GUILLIAME DE LA FLECHERE was born in Noyon, Switzerland, on September 12, 1729. In 1752, with the anglicized name of John Fletcher, he moved to England where the message of John Wesley and the Methodists arrested his attention and his soul. He was ordained a priest in the Church of England (March 1757) and became vicar of Madeley, Shropshire in 1760. He faithfully maintained his post there for the rest of his life.

In 1768 he accepted the position of president of the college at Trevecca, sustained by the Countess of Huntingdon. The college was established to train ministers, but the Countess leaned toward Calvinist predestinarian theology. This brought Fletcher into such conflict that he resigned after a tenure of only three years.

In 1781 Fletcher married a woman well-known for her piety, Mary Bosanquet. From all indications, the marriage was an extremely satisfactory one, as both seemed deeply in love. His wife left a touching, detailed account of her life with him in her own autobiography, *The Life of Mrs. Mary Fletcher* (also published by Schmul Publishing Company).

John Fletcher is perhaps best noted for his *Checks to Antinomianism*, issued the same year he resigned the college presidency (1771). This work set forth the theological views of early Methodists so precisely that it became a standard text for Wesleyans on both sides of the Atlantic.

Fletcher was no armchair theologian, however. His life exemplified the life of holiness so much that he became known far and wide for his saintly mode of living. He attracted the attention of John Wesley himself to the extent the founder of Methodism made it known he intended Fletcher to succeed him in the leadership of the fledgling church.

Such an administration was not to be, however. John Fletcher died before Wesley, on August 14, 1785. His body is buried in the churchyard where he labored so steadfastly. But his gentle influence permeated Methodism in both Britain and America, and today's Wesleyans owe him much for his careful articulation of the doctrine of Christian Perfection.

If you enjoyed *Fletcher on Perfection*, by John Fletcher, you will want these related classic and contemporary books:

Life of Mrs. Mary Fletcher/Moore   #3719

A goldmine of information and insight into the life of John Fletcher's wife. This is an example of consecration too often lacking in our world today, and makes a vast contribution to the body of literature concerned with the "heir apparent" of John Wesley.

Doctrine of Original Sin/J Wesley   #393X

Dr. Richard S. Taylor: "'The doctrine of entire sanctification stands or falls with the doctrine of original sin...' With a new Foreword by Dr. Taylor. For easier reading, we carefully changed Old English words only *to modern English, but* we have not altered the message, personality or structure of any sentence.

Holiness in the Midst of Everyday Life/J Wesley   #3964

John Wesley insists that Perfect Love affects the way we live our daily life. With a new Foreword by Dr. William Kostlevy. For easier reading, we carefully changed Old English words only to modern English, but we have not altered the message or personality of any sentence.

John Wesley & Learning/Byrne   #3611

Examines practical applications of Wesley's demand for life-long education for early Methodists, from Kingswood School to his constant urging for preachers and class leaders to read and learn. Detailed discussion of his curriculum and teaching methods from a respected former seminary professor.

Journal of Charles Wesley   #005N

The sweet singer of the Methodist revival gives unique insights into the great revival that saved England. Informative, devotional, and inspiring.

Sayings and Portraits of John Wesley/Telford #3360

A great reference book of the various portraits of Wesley at different stages of his life, accompanied by short sayings and maxims.

Studies in the Life of John Wesley/Chappell   #2844

The life of Wesley is a source of continuing encouragement, blessing and inspiration. A unique study in many ways and contains information not found in other single volumes.

Wesley on Perfection/JA Wood   #1201

A compilation of everything Wesley wrote in sermons, journals and booklets on holiness.

Wesley's 52 Standard Sermons   #2313

Hardback. The only way to know Wesley's emphasis and teaching is to read his sermons. The 52 Sermons appear as Wesley approved them.

Wesley's Old Testament Notes   #1457

Over two hundred years ago John Wesley took his notes on the O. T. to the printer. One thousand sets were printed. These sets have been collector's items for many years. Schmul Publishing Company is pleased to make them available to Wesleyan scholars again. 3600 pages in 3 volumes.

Wesley's Veterans   #1406

Thirty-five autobiographies of Wesley's greatest preachers and soul winners was written for Mr. Wesley at his request—a rich gold mine of spiritual illustrative material. Seven volumes.

Whitefield & Wesley on the New Birth/Smith #007N

Wesley and Whitefield were almost inseparable as friends beginning from the earliest days of Methodism. They eventually differed greatly on predestination and heart purity yet remained great friends to the end.

Work of the Holy Spirit in the Human Heart/Edwards,Wesley   #3808

Written by the Great Awakening's premiere preacher Jonathan Edwards—abridged by John Wesley! Edwards' insistent call to "holy practice" eventually cost him his pulpit. Wesley was impressed by the summons, but felt it necessary to abridge certain objectionable doctrinal points. Outstanding call to holy living.

Central Idea of Christianity/JPeck   #3905

Takes the position that a pure heart is the central aim of the Christian life. Very logical and scriptural. By one of the five Peck brothers of the 19th Century who became Methodist preachers.

Christian's Manual/Merritt   #3824

In 1825 this book affected Sarah Lankford so deeply she resolved to enter the blessing of Perfect Love. When she founded the famous Tuesday Meetings for the Promotion of Holiness Sarah led her sister, Phoebe Palmer, into the experience of sanctification. Phoebe Palmer went on to become known as the Mother of the Holiness Movement.

Clean Heart/McLaughlin   #2089

The book you need to answer critics of holiness

Defense of Christian Perfection/D Steele   #1643

This is one of Daniel Steele's finest books. A criticism of Dr. James Mudge's "Growth in Holiness Toward Perfection."

Holiness as Understood by Writers of Bible/Beet   #1740

The great scholar examines God's Word with careful exegesis and presents scriptural insights into the life and experience of holiness by writers of the Bible.

Holiness Heart Talks/Clarke, Foster and Peck   #202X

Three great holiness writers talk about "Christian holiness."

Holiness Readings/Various   #0450
General Booth, James Caughey, Amanda Smith, Commissioner Railton, Adam Clarke, John Fletcher, Daniel Steele, and Bishop Peck. Here is a singular compilation for your inspiration and enjoyment.

John Wesley's Concept of Perfection/Cox   #3913
One of the best books of our time. Never dodges the tough questions, and deals with them honestly. Deeply respected by Holiness people everywhere for its integrity and unapologetic orthodox Wesleyan position, this book makes the doctrine plainly understood.

Letters on Sanctification/Hunt   #166X
These rare letters reveal tremendous insights into the holiness experience.

Man's Ascent to God/P Maxey   #3069
This book endeavors to reveal the predicament man is in, how he got into that condition, the way out, the steps he must take to escape eternal damnation and finally make it to the City of God.

Milestone Papers/Daniel Steele   #1538
Spiritual mountaineering. Victory in temptation. The tense studies are standard and classic to Wesleyan students.

Objections to Calvinism/Foster   3743
The classic Arminian response to a Calvinist's attack. Bishop Foster employs formidable logic and scriptural principles. Outstanding!

Pentecost/Brice   #0922
Dr. R. S. Nicholson... "Comments terse and nontechnical...the book is full of challenge and reveals what is trivial and what is abiding relating to the Pentecostal experience."

Perfect Love/JA Wood   #2445

Plain things for those who need them, concerning the doctrine, experience, profession and practice of Christian holiness.

Theology of Holiness/D Clark   #3476

All the way from the Patriarchs to the Apostles—in the Law, the types, the Psalms, the prophets, history, Gospels, epistles—we find that God requires His people to be holy, and to be holy now. By the noted sanctified Quaker.

Treatise on Christian Perfection/Treffrey   #2860

Minister of English Wesleyan Connection joining in 1792. Its arguments are clear-conclusive, its illustrations pertinent-convincing, and its references to human authority rich-varied.
